Money TALK$

Volume Three

Uncut Convos with Financial Experts on
How To Grow, Leverage and Protect Your Assets

Money TALK$

Volume Three

Uncut Convos with Financial Experts on
How To Grow, Leverage and Protect Your Assets

PIERUCCI
PUBLISHING
ELEVATING WORLD CONSCIOUSNESS
THROUGH STORIES

Published by Pierucci Publishing, P.O. Box 2074, Carbondale, Colorado 81623, USA
www.pieruccipublishing.com

Cover design by Stephanie Pierucci
Edited by Russell Womack

Ebook ISBN: 978-1-956257-91-5
Hardcover ISBN: 978-1-956257-92-2

Library of Congress Control Number: 2023919487

Pierucci Publishing books may be purchased in bulk at special discounts for sales promotion, corporate gifts, fund-raising, or educational purposes. Special editions can be created to specifications. For details, contact the Special Sales Department, Pierucci Publishing, PO Box 2074, Carbondale, CO 81623 or Support@ PierucciPublishing.com or toll-free telephone at 1-855-720-1111.

Disclosures:
Information in this publication does not involve the rendering of personalized investment, insurance, tax nor legal advice but is limited to the dissemination of general educational information on financial instruments, products or services. None of the content should be viewed as an offer to buy or sell, or as a solicitation of an offer to buy or sell any of the securities discussed.

A licensed, qualified, investment, insurance, tax or legal professional advisor should always be consulted before implementing any of the options presented. With regards to general investment information, all investment strategies have the potential for profit or loss. Changes in investment strategies, economic conditions, contributions or withdrawals may significantly alter a portfolio's performance. There is no guarantee that any specific investment or strategy will be suitable or profitable for a particular client. Past performance is no guarantee of future success. None of the content should be viewed as an offer to buy or sell, or as a solicitation of an offer to buy or sell any securities discussed.

Dedication

This book is dedicated to my amazing matriarchs:

Great, great grandmothers Addie and Lena

Great Grandmothers Nathelma and Elizabeth

Grandmothers Nathelma and Constance

Mother Dorothy

I carry their names as "Constance Nathelma"...
I carry their blood, hopes, dreams, voice, and legacy.

Constance Craig-Mason
October, 2023

Special Acknowledgments

Money TALK$ Vol III is presented by Dr. Constance Craig-Mason, MRFC® and sponsored by the following companies and organizations.

Special Acknowledgments

Thank you to the following pre-sale supporters and our generous small business partners.

Presale Supporters

Lisa Pierce

Shar Robinson

Tiffany Jeffers

Tiffiney Hall

Dr. Eric Holmes

Davetta Henderson

Tia Harrington

Megan Turek-Green

Danielle Curtis

Kecia Dickerson

Dr. Sanja Rickett-Stinson

Kimberly Daniel-Hopkins

Sultana Jones

Dr. Shannon Harrington

Nikia Pratt

Lisa Moore-Holliday

Nina Sloan

Queen GerVaise Guyton

Tamika Howell

Leslie Giscombe, AAEA

Jerome "Hutch" Hutchinson, Jr. ICABA

Kirby Williams, Advantage Publications

T. Priester, SOBA

Brian J. Olds, BSN

The First Community Bank of Central AL

The Enoch Pratt Free Library of Maryland

Rizwan Rashid, Canada Media Production

Robert "YB" Youngblood, YB Connects

Che Brown, Easy Sales Hub

Dr. Mireille Toulekima Global Leadership

Dupe' Aleru, Davi Creative LLC.

Pastor Phillip Davis, Greater Shiloh Church

LaTecia Yarbrough, iRise Wellness

The PEACES Collective

T. Renee Garner Productions

Through My Lense Consulting

Erica Lane, Global Profit Solutions

Dr. Eric Holmes, The Power of Influence

Small Business Partners

Dr. Adwoa Akhu

Ashleigh Demi Brand

Denoli, LLC.

Oaks of Central PA

Rodney C. Burris

Instill Publishing

Hit The Rest! LLC

Beyond the Salute

AMN Global

L.E.S. Enterprises

The Parenting 411

Barter Black

Afros & Audio

Loose Seeds Media

Hazelbrook Cons

Elizabeth Lieba

Dr. Daniel Moses

The Financial Griot

Dr. David Banks

LaToya Wiggins

Nyteisha Stith

Dr. Lia Abney, DPA

Crystina Cardozo

Ruth Arsenec

Dionne Joi

Dr. Theresa A. Moseley

Treal Ravenel

Brei Endia

Dr. LaToshka Castle

Corlissa Hooks

Monica Reed, The Black Family Magazine

Janelle Jacques, Essence Insurance Agency

Francheska Felder, SwagHer Magazine & Media

Dr. Sharon H. Porter, V&P Lifestyle Magazine & Media

Dr. Jovan Jackson, Good News Financial & Investment Advisors

Adebola Ajao, Empowering Initiatives

Precious L. Williams, Perfect Pitch Group

Jerry Hall, New Millennial Success Academy

Camari Ellis EA, The Philly Tax Team

Omeakio Tucker, Elevate with O, LLC

Acquania Escarne, The Purpose of Money

Naseema McElroy, Financially Intentional Podcast

Lisa Stringer Bailey, Triple M Money Management Matters

Anthony Weaver, About That Wallet, LLC.

Natolie Warren, The Whole Woman Experience

Mercy Arinze Ezeugo, The Complete Woman Show

Dr. Alisa Whyte, Fulfillment Empowerment Network

Charlotte Howard Collins, WWEN

Andrena Phillips, Keep Movin' With Andrena, LLC.

Dr. Catherine Jackson, Optimal Neuroholistic Services

Dr. Nichole Peters, Believe in Your Dreams Productions

Kenyatta Powers-Rucker, KD Powers Consulting

Table of Contents

Foreword
Les Brown

"Money Talks: Uncut Convos with Financial Experts on How to Grow, Leverage and Protect Your Assets" is an insightful book that will help individuals discover the path toward financial wealth. Financial security girdles between employment, inheritance, investments, cultural diversity and awareness, and opportunity. My intention in life has always been to create generational wealth for my children, grandchildren and now my great-grandchildren. And, over time I've learned that a big part of positioning oneself to obtain wealth is not only about intention but also about discipline, focus and perseverance.

Money is not earned in a day nor lost in a moment. People sometimes work their entire life and then transition before they're able to enjoy all of their lifelong earnings. Or, they execute the necessary paperwork to assure their assets are allocated according to their own will and desire. That's why this book is so timely.

Changing how we view money, assets, and wealth is critical to real financial success. And that's exactly what the visionary, Dr. Constance Craig-Mason, and the co-authors accomplish with this book. I recommend reading the insights contained within and getting a copy for someone you love.

As you delve into the advice and guidance offered in this book, take the time to reflect on your own views about money, wealth building, and protecting your assets. Ask yourself: What are my financial goals in the short-term and long-term? Am I living within my means and budgeting effectively? Have I considered different investment options like stocks, real estate, or bonds? Do I have a will and estate plan in place to protect my assets and legacy? Am I continuously learning about personal finance and investment strategies?

Always remember even as it relates to your financial status in life, "Shoot for the moon and if you miss you will still be among the stars". Now is the time to hold yourself accountable for shifting your internal financial conversations and your ongoing financial actions in order to manifest a life you desire.

Dr. Les Brown

About Les Brown
As one of the world's most renowned motivational speakers, Les Brown is a dynamic personality and highly sought after resource in business and professional circles for Fortune 500 CEOs, small business owners, and non-profit and community leaders from all sectors of society looking to expand opportunity. For three decades he has not only studied the science of achievement, but he's mastered it by interviewing hundreds of successful business leaders and collaborating with them in the boardroom translating theory into bottom-line results for his clients. He has received the National Speakers Association coveted Council of Peers Award of Excellence (CPAE) and its most prestigious Golden Gavel Award for achievement and leadership in communication. In addition, Toastmasters International also voted him one of the Top Five Outstanding Speakers Worldwide.

Introduction
Dr. Constance

Hey, it's Dr. Constance here. Let me be the first to welcome you to "the village"- it's a safe space where you can be yourself and express yourself without fear, shame, or wondering if anyone will assume that you "*are having financial challenges*" if they see you engaging with this piece of work or the contributors herein. We don't do that here or in any of the social spaces that we curate to continue engaging with you. So again, welcome– have a seat, take your shoes off, and grab a snack 'cause we want you to take your time and enjoy the stories, insights and perspectives of our contributors.

As the Visionary of this collective, I have partnered with 23 other African American financial thought-leaders from around the world weaving our stories, lessons learned and perspectives within the pillars of how to manifest (mindset), grow, leverage and protect your assets! This book is the golden key that unlocks the door to your economic liberation.

Like a lighthouse in a storm, it guides you from the tempestuous seas of financial insecurity to the calming shores of economic tranquility. It's an invitation to embark on a thrilling journey of financial self-discovery and empowerment: a journey that transforms fears into fortitude and dreams into reality.

Designed specifically with BIPOC families, struggling small business owners, hardworking professionals, and ambitious entrepreneurs in mind, this book tailors its wisdom to resonate with your unique experiences and challenges. Whether you're a parent wrestling with financial stress or a newbie entrepreneur battling the odds, "*Money TALK$ Vol. III*" has the financial wisdom you need.

"Money TALK$ Volume III" is here for those who desire a life of M.O.R.E! It's brimming with tips that will help you intentionally create more great memories, pursue more opportunities, build more healthy reciprocal relationships, and step into more exciting experiences (M.O.R.E). In these pages, you will learn how to navigate the financial world confidently, how to manage your assets and debts like a pro, and how to infuse tradition and innovation for success. Dive in to discover the tools and strategies needed to unlock financial freedom and build a legacy of wealth.

We believe that all sustainable and behavioral change begins in the mind. Therefore, we open this powerful collective with a focus on developing a positive, growth-oriented mindset and healing from financial traumas. We endeavor to teach, equip, empower and inspire BIPOC families, small business owners and professionals to make more, save more, enjoy more and leave more money by prioritizing financial literacy, financial wellness and financial planning.

Positive mindset, along with consistent, intentional money habits combined with the support of knowledgeable, passionate financial experts is a recipe for long term, financial independence and freedom that you deserve.

Dr. Constance

Mindset & Money

Chapter One:
"The Sacred Guardian"

"I understand that money isn't a core value; but money is a reflection of living in your values with purpose and productivity. It is a reflection of being a sacred guardian of my destiny; and doing that well."

ASHLIN PRICE, LMSW, FSW

FINANCIAL CONSULTANT, PREPARE/ ENRICH FACILITATOR...MINDFULLY MOVING TOWARD FINANCIAL FREEDOM

Ashlin is a sought after speaker, certified prepare & enrich marriage facilitator and financial literacy consultant that specializes in providing financial literacy, addressing behaviors related to finances, relationship building and personal development. As the owner of Financial Freedom Enterprises LLC, she has been able to provide services to communities and organizations in need of financial education and strategic planning to improve their personal and professional finances.

Ms. Price possesses a Masters in Social Work from the University of Maryland Baltimore. Her role as a licensed social worker gives her direct experience working with juvenile justice, family investment, addictions, child welfare and mental health/behavioral industries. With all this under her belt, she has been featured on various media platforms to discuss personal and financial health along with wellness

In February 2021, my life changed forever when my brother passed away. My perspective of relationships, interactions, friendships, and even the concept of time changed.

For most people, including myself, February is a month of love, joy and showing gratitude for your partner, spouse, and loved ones with lots of flowers, hugs, smiles, candles, cupid arrows, hearts, and romanticizing. Previously, my Valentine's months were just that: filled with flowers, hugs, gratitude, love, and joy.

In this chapter, I'll show you how I leveraged a tragedy I didn't choose to transmute previously limiting beliefs into empowering lifestyle changes, specifically with regards to my relationship with money.

For whatever reason, the tragedy of my brother passing was part of my divine destiny. I often tell people that this interaction "chose me", even though I didn't, and would never, have chosen to lose my brother. My brother passing away was a smack in the face: everything felt like a tangled mess in my life for that February as well as for many months thereafter. It wasn't the material responsibilities of life insurance, a homegoing service, and supporting my family that overwhelmed me. Those were handled in weeks.. But for months following my brother's passing, the emotional and psychological transformation was stifling.

In the next few minutes, I'll show you how this tragedy turned depression eventually turned out to be a rebirth in my life. I began with this affirmation:

"Tragedy transforms me. I accept all things because I powerfully use all things to my advantage."

The year following my tragedy was filled with confusion, embarrassment, tears, skepticism and forced smiles. However, I was also devoted to the work of building a new relationship with money while grieving. Previously, nobody had taught me how to relate to money in an abundant way. I saw money through one lens, and from only one angle. I had to navigate without a GPS. The principles I was forced to learn through the tragedy weren't nurtured into me by previous life experiences.

Please take a look at this model of the "truth." From each stakeholder's perspective, the image looks completely different. In my life, I was taught to see one aspect of money; money is earned (through toil) to pay bills (barely.) During the year after my tragedy, I learned to see the other angles and facets of money so that I could leverage it better in my life.

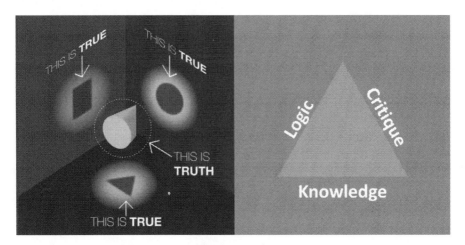

Sadly, I wasn't taught about finances from my parents or from school. Over the years, I have transformed my relationship with money. The communication between me and money was clumsy at first. It was all trial and error for me.

Lesson #1: Humility

For instance, when I was 24 years old I got an apartment. I felt like the bee's knees. However, I also had a car note, insurance, and I was a full-time student. The apartment was the trial. The error was the overwhelming stack of bills I'd acquired. I ended up moving in with a cousin after a few years on my own so that I could leverage my money better.

Thanks to this decision, I became a homeowner at only 28 years old. I went from being strapped, living paycheck-to-paycheck on my own to going to live with my cousin. That humble and wise decision allowed me to pay off debt and save enough money for a down payment on my very own home as a single, self-supporting woman.

Lesson #2: Knowing What I Actually Deserved

The process of becoming a homeowner also taught me something more sobering about society. The prevailing messages include:

"Buy this, you *deserve it*."

However, I learned to play the long game. And I <u>deserved</u> to not succumb to the marketing messages telling me that I deserved to burn my hard-earned money for something I didn't need for somebody's else's profit.

I learned the value of saving for something bigger. I made compromises and sacrifices to save for my home. I didn't buy sneakers, dinners out, or even nice clothes. I worked overtime and saved every spare penny. My entire life became laser-focused on proving to my lender that I could be a responsible homeowner. I was playing the long game.

Theoretically, I always knew the basics of saving money and paying my bills, but I didn't have a relationship with money that empowered me to manifest my dreams. My first apartment is an example of the first time I was challenged to be truly conscious about money.

As Americans, we value independence. But sometimes, that comes at a counterintuitive loss of freedom. The independence I had living on my own in an apartment came at the price of not being able to save money for a house; which can be an investment. I got some bruises along the way. As with so many important life lessons, most people don't get serious until they're forced to. Too often, you don't open up the map until you're already lost. My life's work is to be that money compass or money GPS for my clients.

Lesson #3: I Heal My Relationship With Money Because I Love My Family

Shortly after my brother passed, my family and I were at the funeral home discussing how much a casket would cost, how much insurance money we had, if there would be flower arrangements, what decision we would make on colors for all of the above, and trying to figure out who the beneficiaries were for his assets. We didn't know how many policies my brother had in place, what date we wanted for his homegoing service, or what insurance was out there at all.

I wondered who was contributing to the service and how they were contributing. Somehow in that moment I assumed that it would be taken care of, wouldn't it? And by whom? Certainly not by me.

The more my family and I discussed the details of the service, the more we realized that we didn't have the money to pay for it. I was gobsmacked. The question of a possible "Go Fund Me" came up; perhaps people would donate to help pay for the funeral service? The very thought caused shame and embarrassment for me because I had already been a financial literacy consultant at that time. And yet… my own family didn't have a plan in place?

Family members indeed contributed money to assist in having a proper homegoing service without the Go Fund Me, but I weathered an ego death fueled by the literal death of somebody I loved so dearly. You don't walk away from such an experience without being changed. It taught me that if you really love your family, you will not let them suffer the way my family and I suffered that day.

You need a money mindset reboot STAT.

At the funeral home that day I slowly stood up and backed away from the table where my family sat, steadying myself by clenching the back of a chair next to me. I was dizzy with frustration, confusion, anger and what felt like a paralyzing weight on each shoulder. As I ambled towards a door, my feet shuffled beneath me as though I was moving through mud. Something had to give. I surrendered my old self that day and vowed that I wouldn't put back pieces in that same puzzle again; I'd wash away my old mindset and become new. Now that is something both me and my family deserved.

Above all, I knew I could never let my family be in a situation where they didn't have the funds to pay for something as simple as a homegoing service. The passing of my brother left my nieces and nephews without a father and their children without a grandfather. It left my mother without a son, and left me and my sister without a brother. It left my cousins and so many members of our community without a friend.

My depression went deeper than "money mindset." I begged God to bring my brother back to me. I vowed to go to church every Sunday and be a servant to anybody who needed me. I'd be His ambassador and share His love. I would go anywhere and do anything. "Please God, just bring him back," I prayed.

Lesson #4: A Good Relationship With Money Brings Life & Purpose

God didn't raise my brother, but he raised me. That depression fueled a process of evaluating my own relationship with money. As God delivered me from the depression, he lifted my perspective high above my circumstances. Suddenly, I was pregnant with purpose; visualizing an emergence out of my fog into the light of positivity and prosperity. I began declaring breakthroughs over my financial house and abundance beyond living paycheck-to-paycheck. In fact, I've written a 30-day affirmations guide to mentor others through the process of manifesting breakthroughs in their lives starting with their money mindset.

I understand that money isn't a core value; but money is a reflection of living in your values with purpose and productivity. It is a reflection of being a sacred guardian of your destiny; and doing that well.

When we are in a state of struggle with money, it triggers survival instincts such as fight or flight. In this state, we are not as present with the people we love. We may fall into the temptation of addiction. We might not have the energy to run around with our kids. We may suffer anxiety that disrupts everything from sleep cycles to our productivity at work. Money isn't as important as air to breathe; but it fuels a beautiful life. When you have enough; you're free to flow through life with elegance, grace, generosity and abundance. But like a fish out of water; if there is no money, you are drowning.

In this way I teach my clients to come face to face with money by defining it, respecting it, and appreciating it with care. This is predicated on your relationship with yourself. Your relationship with yourself precedes everything; if you haven't given yourself permission to be in abundance, you won't call in that abundance. When you embrace money wisdom, a rising tide lifts all boats. Your friendships, love relationships, health, and, of course, finances will all prosper.

Just like a parent teaching children the family business, your relationship with money begins in childhood. What we see in our families we will model in our lives. A mother in constant distress about not paying bills, being fired, losing income, or getting the lights turned off will create a relationship of stress with money. A household with anxiety around money affects children. In that house, money is a bully or even an abuser. When you reset your relationship with money, money is more like a generous benefactor opening up doors of opportunity for your family at every turn.

A relationship of respect and love with money will beget a fruitful and peaceful home. When the belief is that money is a reflection of hard work, even the work will become easier because the reward is assured. The equation becomes logical and the anxiety, depression, or chaotic worrying that consumes the mind plagued with bad money beliefs will be at peace. From that state of peace comes more prosperity.

Lesson #5: Money Principles to Transform Your Relationship with Money Starting Today

My mentor in professional money coaching is Reeta Wolfsohn from the Center of Financial Social Work. One of the core models in my practice comes from Reeta's "The Four Financial Social Work Core Principles of Financial Healing" methodology. These four principles include:

1. Rethinking and Restructuring Relationship with Money and The Self
2. Developing Healthier Financial Habits
3. Making Friends with Money
4. Increasing Financial Knowledge

When I begin working with my clients, we work through all four Principles over the course of several months together, starting with my own financial well-being model.

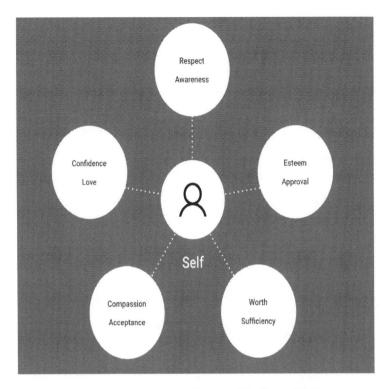

Financial Well Being Model Provided By Reeta Wolfhson

Is Money A Bully or A Benefactor?

As illustrated in the story earlier about money being a bully in a home vs. a benefactor, the relationship you have with your money begins at childhood and evolves over the course of a lifetime. No one comes out of their mother's womb being money savvy and knowing all the tricks of money. Our money habits are influenced by how we were raised. Whether we grew up in a household where we had discussions about money or we did not have discussions about money, whether money was scarce or it was abundant. It all shapes and molds our reality.

As we grow up, outside factors influence how we see money and the significance it has in our lives. Money has a purpose. Money *fuels* your purpose. Rather than money being the stick, start to frame it as the carrot. It isn't a punisher, it is the reward of living and being in your purpose. Money affects our feelings, attitudes, perspectives, and beliefs. The more we nurture a positive relationship with money where we have the courage to communicate with money confidently, the better the results of that relationship; i.e. more wealth.

Money as the benefactor may look like the moment when we receive a paycheck or a tax return deposited into our accounts; we feel excited. Maybe you receive a generous gift. You may feel like you're floating on cloud nine; like no one can influence your mood. Having that prosperity or nest egg, even for a short time, can make you feel invincible.

Money as the bully is that moment when you must decide between putting gas in your car or buying groceries for your family. In that scenario, you have made money stressful and overbearing. You have chosen to let money be the bully. It has even been said that money is the number one stressor in people's lives. Looking around you, would you disagree?

Why don't we feel excited or like we're "floating on cloud nine" when we only have $15 in our accounts compared to $1,500? Primarily, that's because we've allowed money to determine our worth. Most financial struggles have less to do with how much money a person has but more to do with how they feel when they have or do not have the money. Do you still feel valuable, worthy, and deserving when you only have $15 in your bank account?

When having conversations with people about their finances, I've noticed that money conversations bring out more emotions than other subjects. Even more than questions about career satisfaction, dating, or health status, people who don't have a good relationship with money are triggered by it. Money woes regularly trigger depression, anxiety, isolation, PTSD, and embarrassment. If a person is already stressed or anxious, financial stress can often be the proverbial straw that breaks the camel's back.

The Five Behaviors of Money

There are five things every person does with money. These include:

1. Spend
2. Save
3. Share
4. Earn
5. Borrow

The relationship you have with yourself and your money determines your financial behavior in each of these five categories. What you do with your money motivates your financial circumstances. For example, think about how you **spend** your money and fill in the blanks below.

How Does Money Manifest In Your Life?

THE 5 BEHAVIORS OF MONEY

Answer these questions to get a pulse of your money behaviors.

1 How much do you save?

2 How do you earn money?

3 Do you share it with friends or family?

4 Do you share too much or too little?

5 Do you repay what you borrow?

6 Do your debts saddle you with anxiety?

7 Do you visualize how to make your money work for you? And how?

Once you are able to attack and answer these questions bravely, you can now transform money from the bully to the benefactor. When you get your money relationship straight, you shift your perspective from dollars and cents to habits and actions which beget peace and prosperity.

The same qualities you want your best friend to have are the same qualities your money should have. Reliable, honest, dependable, sense of humor and respectful. Some say money is the root of all evil… but is money the root of all evil? …Or it is our behaviors that contribute to the saying?

When money is considered the "enemy," the resulting relationship is likely to be negative. But when money is considered a "friend," it is respected, appreciated, and loved.

Money treats you how you treat it. Consider money as an enhancement. Don't allow yourself to be pressured to buy things on-demand, but consider leveraging your extra money to serve and bless others. Above all, speak positively to your money.

I leave you with the four affirmations I live by daily, taken from my book "Affirming My Value: 31 Days of Financial Affirmations and Elevations."

FINANCIAL
Freedom
ENTERPRISE
FINANCIAL LITERACY

FOUR MONEY AFFIRMATIONS

YOU ARE WORTHY, VALUABLE, DESERVING AND WORTH THE INVESTMENT.

NO MATTER THE CIRCUMSTANCE OR HOW BAD THINGS MAY LOOK YOU HAVE THE POWER TO REWRITE YOUR STORY, TO CULTIVATE A NEW RELATIONSHIP.

WHAT YOU THINK AND WHAT YOU SAY TRANSLATES INTO YOUR REALITY.

YOU'RE NEVER TOO OLD OR YOUNG TO LEAVE A LEGACY OF GENERATIONAL WEALTH NOT ONLY FINANCES BUT EDUCATION, PROPERTY, AND LOVE.

FROM THE BOOK "AFFIRMING MY VALUE: 31 DAYS OF FINANCIAL AFFIRMATIONS AND ELEVATIONS"

Together, I hope we can rewrite your financial legacy starting today with your beliefs and the relationship you have with money. Although I still mourn the loss of my brother, I am grateful today that he has inspired me to be a sacred guardian not just of my own financial health, but the health of others, too.

Chapter Two:

"The Three E's of Rewiring Your Money Mindset"

RAHKIM SABREE, CFEI®, RFC®

FINANCIAL COACH AND CONSULTANT

Rahkim Sabree is the author of the best-selling book "Financially Irresponsible", a Forbes columnist, and financial coach and consultant with over a decade of financial services and financial wellness industry experience.

His work has been seen or published in many large publications, TED, and more. Rahkim focuses on the intersection of money, mental health, and race focusing on things like financial trauma, financial therapy, and financial empowerment for people who look like him.

For more on Rahkim visit RahkimSabree.com or connect on social media @RahkimSabree.

I recently came across a rebuttal to the popular phrase, "money is the root of all evil" that read, "the lack of money is the root of all evil," and I had to pause. So much of the value we as a society place on how much money we have (or don't have) is based on how much money we see that someone else has. While a great tool for financial goal setting, how we justify what we have, don't have, need, want, and can't live without financially has less to do with the amount of money we earn or keep and more to do with what we believe about money, what we believe about ourselves, whether or not we deserve money, and how we are supposed to use it.

My name is Rahkim Sabree and at the time of this writing, I have over a decade of industry experience in financial services and financial education. While most of my work has been centered around the financial fundamentals of budgeting, saving, investing, and building credit, I recently stumbled upon a path that is arguably more important than all of that. I discovered financial therapy.

Whether you pick up books on personal development or personal finance, attend lectures and seminars, or watch videos and podcasts, you'll hear advice that often tells you what you should be doing with your money, how you should be thinking, that you should have "an abundance mindset", that you should spend less than you earn and that you should save a portion of your income for a rainy day. If you've ever consumed content like this you may feel inspired and encouraged to do each of these things until you hit a wall in trying to figure out exactly how.

How do I exit survival mode?

How do I change my scarcity mindset?

How do I prioritize my savings when emergencies keep coming up?

This content often leaves you feeling guilt, shame, and frustration about the fact that it seems like everyone else can do it, but you can't. However, the truth is that you can, it's just that none of these practices and ideas address the root of what your issue is in the first place and they don't teach you how to heal.

The link between our beliefs about money and our behaviors is a powerful and often overlooked aspect of our financial lives. Our beliefs shape our mindset, which in turn influences our actions and decisions when it comes to money. Understanding this connection is crucial for developing a holistic approach to money that takes into account not only our financial knowledge but also our culture, background, experience, and behavior. So when we experience financial stress, financial anxiety, or financial trauma, it can negatively influence what we believe about the role of money in our lives creating a domino effect that impacts our mindset and behaviors.

Financial trauma is any instance, observed or experienced, that has a negative impact on the way you view, interact with, or believe about money. Arguably, most of the mainstream approaches to financial education leverage guilt, shame, and fear to drive home the value of knowing and executing on financial fundamentals which assume that everyone is starting with the same levels of access to education and resources. This approach ignores the burdens of generational and lived trauma that acts as a barrier to perceived success. Worse still is when all efforts by the consumer are aligned to checking off the boxes of what the educators tell them are markers for success, and yet they are still left feeling unfulfilled and confused about what's next.

When we examine our beliefs about money, we start to uncover deep-seated attitudes and assumptions that have been ingrained in us since childhood. These beliefs may be influenced by our upbringing, our cultural and societal norms, and the experiences we've had with money throughout our lives. For example, if we grew up in an environment where money was scarce and there was a constant struggle to make ends meet, we might develop a scarcity mindset that affects our ability to save and invest.

On the other hand, if we were surrounded by abundance and never had to worry about money, we might develop a sense of entitlement or a lack of financial discipline. These beliefs about money can be limiting and self-sabotaging, preventing us from reaching our financial goals and creating a healthy relationship with money.

Many believe that money is evil or that we don't deserve to be wealthy or that wealth is a barrier the system won't allow for us to penetrate unless we "sell our soul". In turn, we may unconsciously push away opportunities for financial success or engage in self-destructive financial behaviors. Our beliefs can also shape our spending habits, leading us to make impulsive purchases or overspend to fill emotional voids.

To develop a holistic approach to money, we need to first become aware of our beliefs and how they influence our financial behaviors. This requires introspection and self-reflection. We can start by asking ourselves questions like:

What do I believe about money?
Where did these beliefs come from?
How do these beliefs impact my financial decisions?

By exploring these questions, we can begin to challenge and reframe our limiting beliefs.

Within my practice of financial coaching using techniques from financial therapy and financial counseling I discuss a framework I refer to as the 3 E's;

Exposure
Education
Execution

Rewiring our brains financially may require being exposed to something we are not used to. When we see that it's possible, we can start to ask how we can make this thing possible for ourselves.

However, changing our beliefs is not enough. We also need to develop financial knowledge and skills that align with our new mindset. This involves **exposure** to wisdom about budgeting, saving, investing, and other financial fundamentals. That is why the next step in this framework is education.

It's essential to **educate** ourselves about personal finance and seek out resources that provide practical guidance on how to manage money effectively. By combining our newfound knowledge with our transformed beliefs, we create a solid foundation for making informed financial decisions and setting realistic goals for the future.

Once we have improved our mindset and gained financial knowledge, the next crucial step is **executing** on that knowledge. The execution phase can be both scary and difficult, especially for those who have experienced financial trauma in the past. The fear of making mistakes or repeating past financial failures can be overwhelming, causing hesitation and resistance to taking action.

Financial trauma can resurface during the execution phase because it brings us face-to-face with our past experiences and triggers old wounds. It may manifest as anxiety, self-doubt, or even a fear of success. The patterns and behaviors that developed as a result of past financial trauma may resurface, making it challenging to break free from those patterns and establish new, healthy financial habits.

It's important to recognize that this stage of execution is where the real transformation happens. It's where we put our newfound knowledge into practice and actively work towards our financial goals. However, it's equally important to approach this phase with patience, self-compassion, and a willingness to confront and heal any remaining financial trauma.

During the execution phase, seeking support from a financial therapist, coach, or mentor can be invaluable. They can provide guidance, accountability, and a safe space to process and work through any financial trauma that may arise. Additionally, building a community or a support network of friends, peers, and family members who are also on a similar financial journey can offer encouragement and understanding.

It's crucial to remember that executing on financial knowledge is a process, and setbacks or challenges may occur along the way. It's normal to encounter obstacles, make mistakes, or face unexpected financial emergencies. But by continuing to learn, adapt, and persevere, we can navigate through these challenges and build resilience in the face of adversity.

Through the execution phase, we have an opportunity to rewrite our financial narrative, heal from past traumas, and create a new and empowered relationship with money. It's a courageous and necessary step on our path toward financial well-being. By acknowledging and addressing any financial trauma that surfaces during this phase, we can break free from the cycle of fear and limitation and move towards a more secure and prosperous future.

I would be remiss if I didn't highlight the one variable in financial trauma discussions that specifically impact people who look like me.

Financial trauma for Black Americans is deeply rooted in the historical context of systemic racism, beginning with the atrocities of slavery and continuing through the persistent inequalities that exist today. This aspect of financial trauma is intertwined with a larger generational trauma that has shaped the experiences of Black individuals and communities. It has led to a deep-seated mistrust in financial institutions and systems, as they have historically perpetuated and reinforced racial disparities.

Acknowledging the impact of generational trauma is crucial in understanding the complexities of financial trauma for Black Americans. From the denial of economic opportunities and property ownership during slavery to the discriminatory practices in housing, employment, and lending that persisted throughout Jim Crow and beyond, the systemic barriers have hindered wealth accumulation and economic mobility for generations.

That is the premise behind the work I do. Together, we can unravel the complexities of financial trauma, challenge systemic barriers, and empower you to build a healthier relationship with money. Your journey toward financial well-being starts here. To learn more visit my website at www.rahkimsabree.com .

Chapter Three:

"From Broke and Broken To Financially at Peace"

RAQUEL CURTIS, MBA

INTERNATIONAL MONEY MANAGEMENT COACH

My name is Raquel Curtis. I am a keynote speaker who facilitates workshops for women, community leaders, entrepreneurs, and students on the importance of financial literacy and business ownership.

I have been featured on Business Insider, Parents Magazine, Fox Soul, Bloomberg Radio, Sirius XM radio, The CW Network, Fincon, The Table with Anthony Oneal and a host of other write ups and podcasts.

Within 2 years I have grown a following of over 100k on Instagram and nearly 80k on TikTok with high interaction and engagement rates.

My self-published book "Mastering Your Money Mindset" digs deep into the readers personal relationship with money, identifying their triggers and helps the reader create healthy boundaries around those triggers for financial success. "Mastering Your Money Mindset" has sold over 1,000 copies in 7 countries with raving 5 star reviews.

Life happens, and when it does, we have two options; We can either fold to the pressure or fight through the storm. For the longest time, I only associated money with being a means to pay bills and enjoy life with the remaining amount in my account.

My relationship with money was simple, I looked forward to paydays and would struggle the week before my next pay period. I was in a cycle of living it up and barely living. I spent so much time ignoring my debt and focused solely on enjoying my money.

My relationship with money was a lot like my past relationships in life…. a mess.

I remember when I lost my retail gym due to a car accident that left me unable to work for a year. With three daughters, we struggled significantly to make ends meet. We were reduced from two incomes coming into the home down to one. But the bills did not change. Once I was able to return to work again, I fought hard to work any kind of job that would bring additional income into the house. But no matter how hard I worked, I had nothing to show for it.

Being broke SUCKED! I was constantly stressed and I was experiencing unwanted weight loss, depression and anxiety. There were days when I wouldn't know if the utility company was driving by our house to service a neighbor or cut off our power. The worst part is that even while feeling all of this, I would put on the biggest "smiley face" for everyone else. At my worst moments, no one could tell. But honestly, I felt like I was dying inside.

Sound like a familiar feeling? Like you'd almost rather pretend the problems weren't there than deal with them?

I was spending without regard. Focused on immediate gratification and just trying to enjoy my money because I felt like I worked too hard and deserved to spend it. But short-term gratification wasn't doing anything to the long-term problem I created.

Eventually I told myself I needed to get it together so I started watching YouTube videos, buying planners, and downloading all the free templates I could. I would go through this cycle of being motivated and making slight progress, to being unmotivated and ending up right back at square one.

I had to realize that, eventually, if those resources were working for everyone else and not me... Then the problem was me.

One day I was so frustrated with myself that I ripped my budget into pieces and started thinking about money from a different perspective. I stopped looking at the numbers and started reflecting on the decisions I'd made with money in the past. Doing this led me down a new path.

Determined to get to the root of why I continually operated the same way with money year over year, I began to wonder: *How did I get to this place with my money? What caused it? Where did my relationship with money start?*

How your childhood affected your relationship with money.

Have you ever heard the saying:

"Be careful how you treat your children because they will grow up to date someone who is just like the way you treated them?"

Everything that you were taught about healthy and unhealthy relationships stems from your parents and the environment in which you were raised. Growing up you may have heard wise elders caution that, "your spouse will be similar to how your mother or father treated you."

If your parent relationship was either abusive or neglectful, then your own first relationship is more than likely going to be similar. The same holds true for a loving and supportive relationship. Loving and supportive parents generally raise children who expect loving and supportive partners. This happens because our values are subconsciously and consciously conditioned. The way our parents treated us or behaved around us trained our minds to believe this is how we were supposed to be treated and how we were supposed to behave.

There are certain red flags that someone who was raised in a neglectful or abusive household would not be able to recognize. This is because those hurtful behaviors would be perceived as being the norm, whereas someone raised in a loving and caring home would acknowledge those behaviors as being toxic.

Red flags do not register as unhealthy until you make a conscious decision to acknowledge that those behaviors are harmful and are no longer serving you. Once you become aware of this, you then have the ability to make a conscious effort and determine who and what you attract in your life.

Just like you were conditioned with people, you were also conditioned with money. I like to believe that we are consciously and subconsciously conditioned on how we operate with our money based on how our environment/parents projected their views, thoughts, feelings, and actions with money onto us.

How your parents talked to you about money growing up, mattered. How they spoke to one another about money mattered. How they acted when they did or didn't have money mattered, and it all played a huge part in the way that you view, feel, think, and operate with money today. It also plays a major part in how you project your views, thoughts, and feelings about money onto other people. Our pasts play significant parts in the way we operate with money as adults.

Let's take a moment to reflect on our childhood and how that may have contributed to how we view, feel and think about money today. I suggest sitting alone in a quiet place and playing some meditation music while completing this exercise. Please allow yourself the space to sink into your memories and emotions. Once you are settled with calming music in a place with no distractions, please answer the following questions:

*How does your past influence
your wealth today?*

YOUR MONEY INHERITANCE

Let's take a moment to reflect on our childhood and how that may have contributed to how we view, feel and think about money today. I suggest sitting alone in a quiet place and playing some meditation music while completing this exercise. Please allow yourself the space to sink into your memories and emotions. Once you are settled with calming music in a place with no distractions, please answer the following questions:

1   What is your first memory of money?

2   When did you first learn about the importance of saving money?

3   What emotions did money trigger in your home?

4   What did you spend your first paycheck on?

5   Did you have a savings account when you graduated from high school? What about college? How much and for what did you save it?

As children we were taught to be kind and treat others with respect. We were taught this Golden Rule about our social interactions with people, but we were not taught a Golden Rule about our interactions with money. How ironic is it that money would soon become the foundation of our livelihood?

As a child you may have been told to "stay out of grown folks business" when it comes to money, or bills. That as long as you had a roof over your head, clothes on your back, and food in your stomach that you didn't need to worry about anything.

While certain phrases they've said might have gotten you out of their business and kept you in a child's place, it probably did more harm than good. You respectfully remained in a child's place until you became an adult and later learned about money. And that first lesson may have been established through debt. 1.6 trillion Americans are in student loan debt according to the U.S. Department of Education as of March 31, 2021.

Most of us didn't establish a relationship with money until we already owed somebody and were forced to swim upstream instead of with the current.

Now, as an adult, do you ever catch yourself saying things that you have heard your parents say? Or acting like them in certain ways?

It's time to get back to playing your meditation music and think back a bit more.

Money Blessings & Wounds

REWRITING MONEY STORIES

1   My first memory of how my father (or father figure) managed money was...

_____

_____

2   My father taught me _____ about money:

_____

_____

3   My first memory of how my mother (or mother figure) managed money was...

_____

_____

4   How did they talk to each other about money?

_____

5   CIRCLE ONE: Money was NEVER/SOMETIMES/ALWAYS a reason my parents argued growing up?

6   If so, what is an argument that you remember?

_____

7   Where was the value placed growing up? (Family, Appearance, Material Things, etc.)

_____

Money Blessings & Wounds

REWRITING MONEY STORIES

1 Growing up, did your parents always work hard for money and live paycheck to paycheck? Or were they financially well-off and their lifestyle reflected that? Please explain...

_____

_____

2 I have learned that over the years my parent/parent's relationship with money affected me into adulthood because....

_____

_____

3 So far, my current relationship with money has cost me.....

_____

_____

4 If I do not change my current relationship with money, I stand to lose....

_____

_____

5 If I do make a change I stand to gain.....

_____

_____

You just took a deep dive into your past and have probably uncovered somethings that you hadn't taken the time to think about before.

It is very important that you identify what is and is not serving you so that you can prevent yourself from projecting those same limiting views, thoughts, and feelings about money onto your child(ren). If you want to build generational wealth, it starts with what you are instilling in them today.

Whether you have children or not, it is important that you recognize what your money triggers are, so that you can create healthy boundaries around those triggers and when they present themselves, you are not tempted to impulsively spend your money.

From what I have learned over my time as a banker and a money coach is that there are two sides of money that people generally fall on.

One side: You may have grown up in a household where your parents struggled and did the best they could to provide, but because their financial habits were poor, money was always tight. This may have created a scarcity mindset, where you're afraid to lose the money you have, and in turn, can never enjoy it. If not, then maybe you have developed a live it up mindset, where you never had access to money so now you're always spending it when you can.

The other side: You may have been raised in a household where everything you needed and/or wanted was provided for you, so you never learned to value your money. Now you find yourself struggling as an adult, to maintain the standard of living that your parents created for you. Unfortunately, you now lack the value attachment to respect money enough to make it happen.

Today, I am a successful international money management coach who has helped thousands of womens with their relationship with money. But, looking back, I promise you, being in this position is something I didn't even dream of once! This all happened because I got clear on my relationship with money, I took immediate action, and I gave myself grace in my growth. Moving forward in this book I want you to offer yourself grace. In order to build a brighter financial future we have to remove the financial bandaid we've placed on ourselves for so many years and dig into the root of where it all started.

Chapter Four:
"The Two Elements of an Effective Legacy"

MARCELLA MOLLON-WILLIAMS, BFA™

Co-Founder and Behavioral Financial Advisor™

 Legacy Builder group

Marcella Mollon-Williams combines her passion for personal development and legacy building as a licensed Behavioral Financial Advisor and co-founder of Legacy Builder Group, LLC, a holistic coaching and investment firm helping families build wealth with purpose.

She is also a Certified Master Mindset and Cognitive Behavioral Coach, as well as a Certified Flexibility Coach. With over 15 years of experience and a leading voice in the behavioral finance industry, Marcella provides a scientific approach to behavioral discipline that guides first generation 6 and 7+ figure earning households in consistently experiencing financial certainty by eliminating mental restraints around money and developing the behavior to grow and maintain a multi-generational family legacy. Marcella has received numerous awards and recognition in finance and entrepreneurship and has been featured on several media publications, radio, and television such as The Wall Street Journal, U.S. News and World Report, TLC and NPR.

Money TALK$

I want you to take in what I am about to tell you. Say it out loud or in your internal voice. Are you ready?

Legacy is how other people will experience my existence.

Just sit with that for a moment. There are countless ways in which our existence can be experienced by others, while we are alive and after we are gone. We have all experienced the lives of relatives who have left an impression within us; from grandma's famous casserole recipe that ensures the family returns home for the holidays to the financial inheritance you received but were completely unaware of until the passing of that dear loved one. While there are numerous ways we may benefit from the experiences of family members and other influential people in our lives, there are also many experiences that have left others broke and broken.

You can see, by the influence that others have had on your life, that you are capable of making a profound impact in the lives of others. Yes, you. You are just that powerful. Every single day, for the rest of your life, you will *choose* between a negligent or intentional existence, until you *decide* to create an effective legacy.

The Two Elements of An Effective Legacy
If you knew me prior to 2019, (I mean, really knew me. Not that social media "I know her" stuff), then you would have noticed a major shift in my behavior in the following years.

Prior to 2019, I was annoyingly indecisive and painfully undisciplined. As a business owner and financial professional, I had to make decisions all the time and I could make many of those decisions based on my knowledge of the circumstances and my experience. The problem came when knowledge and experience was lacking. When those two elements were not present, a breeding ground of doubt would plague me and when it was time to make a simple decision, I struggled with the fear of the idea of making the wrong decision.

On top of my indecisiveness was my undisciplined behavior. I suffered from Start/Stop Syndrome (That's not a real syndrome, I just made that up but it makes sense in my head). You know- you start one thing for a while and then stop. Then you start something else and stop that as well. Maybe you go back to the first thing, give it a shot for a while and then stop again. That became the story of my life. It took me seven years to get through a One-Year Bible, due to my SSS condition.

The catalyst for my change began on September 28, 2019. For the next 21 months, I would be taken through the most transformative journey of my life; one that would teach me to develop the behavior that will build my desired legacy.

An effective legacy requires two elements:

- A definite **decision** to achieve the intended outcome,
- And the dedicated **discipline** to remain consistent.

When you combine these two elements, you become determined to operate in a way that will shift the trajectory of your life - you will operate with **intentionality**.

Resolve To Make A Change

I woke up September 28, 2019, ready to celebrate my 45th birthday. I am not a big birthday person but I figured it was a milestone year that I should acknowledge. As I began to move about the day, a migraine began to set in. At that moment, I **decided** that I was sick and tired of feeling sick and tired. I often struggled with up to four migraines a month, plus chronic fatigue, which was something I dealt with since I was a child. I was probably the only kid that loved naps.

Decision: come to a resolution in the mind as a result of consideration.

With one simple decision, I resolved to make a change in my life. I knew that in order to change my behavior, especially that pesky Start/Stop Syndrome, I had to do something that would challenge me both physically and mentally. The idea was a revelation to me. A SIDE SPLIT CHALLENGE!

Let me make this clear, I am, nor was I ever a naturally flexible person. A split was something I was never able to do. I came close when I was 16 years old, but never gave it another thought after I pulled my hamstring during a dance routine in high school.

So there I was, 45 years old with 29 years of tight muscles and joints, about to embark on this crazy fitness challenge.

What does this have to do with Money?

First let's address the elephant in the chapter. This is a financial book and except for the words financial inheritance in the beginning of this chapter, I have not mentioned money at all. Well, that was intentional. As a licensed Behavioral Financial Advisor and Certified Cognitive Behavioral Coach, my job is to help my clients manage their savings and investment behavior. Why? Because numerous studies have shown that it's our behavior that negatively impacts our finances, the most. I have been working with clients on elevating their money mindset for 11+ years and I've seen the behavioral connections in their lives. Money is an amplifier. It brings out who we already are. It will amplify our best habits and our worst behavior.

While I was good at what I did as a financial coach/advisor and had the education and knowledge to support my clients, I did not always practice what I preached. Sometimes, I felt like that doctor, outside the ER on his break, smoking a cigarette. He knows smoking is a bad habit and terrible for his health. It's a classic case of cognitive dissonance (when what you want or believe does not line up with what you do) and there are multiple reasons for this disconnect. I just needed to figure out what was the reason for mine.

This is what I learned: my indecisiveness and undisciplined behavior was holding me back from building the legacy that I truly desired. When I became crystal clear on how I wanted other people (my family, community, clients, team, etc.) to experience my existence, and developed the consistent behavior around decisiveness and discipline that would get me there, my world changed.

A Framework for Freedom

For almost two years, I was taken on a journey that would completely shift my mindset. Remember that breeding ground for doubt I spoke about earlier? Well, that was replaced by confidence. Every decision became intentional. I began experiencing extraordinary growth in every area of my life (finance, fitness, family and faith) and on June 24, 2021, I accomplished my full side split, twenty-one months later.

I was so excited to finally achieve my physical goal. However, by the time I did, it was already clear to me that this journey was never about the split. This entire challenge was about creating a framework for freedom. I believe that at the core of each of us, money is the tool we use to access our true desire - freedom.

There are habits and behaviors that you have tolerated from yourself that are holding you back from living and leaving an effective legacy. Maybe other people planted thoughts in your head that diminished your value and, eventually, you accepted them. Perhaps the challenges of life created a breeding ground of doubt that you try to fill with more degrees and certifications.

I am here to tell you that YOU are a Powerful Legacy Builder! I know you can feel it because it is the reason you are reading this book. (trust me, there are a lot of people that would not touch a financial book unless you paid them to read it.)

Now, get clarity on what you are building. Make a list of all the ways you want people to experience your existence, both now and after you are gone. Don't limit yourself. Then, make a definitive decision to achieve one goal at a time with dedicated discipline. By intentionally operating within this framework, you will develop the behavior that will build the legacy your descendants will be talking about for generations to come.

Chapter Five:
"The Treasure House Within You"

OTIS TOGBAH TARWOE

**Author | Serial Entrepreneur | International Speaker/Trainer | Leadership Expert |
Global Influencer | CEO - Tarwoe Global Consulting LLC**

Otis Togbah Tarwoe is Africa's Premier International Speaker, Project
and Business Management consultant, Policy and Development
analyst, youth activist, Leadership and personal development coach,
and a certified Communication Expert from Kigali, Rwanda.

He is the Author of two distinguish transformational Books "Unique
Potential of a Pragmatic Leader", and "The Undefeated You" that
straightly focuses on Leadership and executing your God-given
purpose.

Within you lies a treasure house of unlimited potential and possibilities. It's up to you to unlock the doors and discover the infinite wealth of talents, strengths, and dreams waiting to be unleashed. The idea that we all have a treasure house within us may seem like a cliché, but it is a profound truth that is often overlooked in the pursuit of external success and validation.

The truth is that we all have unique gifts, talents, and abilities that are waiting to be unlocked and unleashed. Whether it's a creative talent, a knack for problem-solving, or a natural charisma, we all have something special within us that can make a positive impact on the world around us. However, unlocking our inner treasure house requires more than just the right mindset, thinking, and a can-do attitude. It requires a mindset shift that goes beyond the superficial and taps into the deeper aspects of who we are as human beings. This mindset shift involves recognizing that our value and worth as individuals do not come from external sources, such as our job title, bank account balance, or social status.

Instead, our value comes from within, from the essence of who we are as unique and valuable creations of God. One of the most powerful biblical stories that illustrates this truth is the parable of the talents, which can be found in Matthew 25:14–30. In this story, a wealthy man goes on a journey and entrusts his three servants with different amounts of money according to their abilities. The first servant is given five talents, the second is given two talents, and the third is given one talent.

The first two servants invest their talents and double their money, while the third servant buries his talent in the ground. When the master returns, he commends the first two servants for their faithfulness and resourcefulness and rewards them with even greater responsibilities. However, he rebukes the third servant for his fear and lack of initiative and takes away his talent.

The lesson of this parable is clear: we all have different talents and abilities and we are responsible for using them to the best of our ability. The first two servants were not given more talents because they were more valuable or worthy than the third servant, but because they had the mindset and courage to invest their talents and take risks. In contrast, the third servant allowed fear and self-doubt to hold him back, and as a result, he missed out on the opportunity to grow and thrive.

In addition to the above Biblical story, there are also practical steps that we can take to unlock our inner treasure house that ultimately results in manifesting financial security and independence. One of the most important steps is to cultivate a growth mindset, which involves the belief that our abilities and talents can be developed through hard work and dedication.

Another important step is to set clear goals and take action toward them. This involves identifying what truly matters to us and setting specific, measurable, achievable, relevant, and time-bound (SMART) goals that will help us achieve our desired outcomes.

What exactly is the treasure house within you?

In modern times, the idea of the treasure house within you has become more relevant than ever. With the increasing demands of modern life, many people are searching for ways to tap into their inner potential and find meaning and purpose in their lives.

Whether you are seeking personal growth, career success, or simply a more financially fulfilling life, understanding and harnessing the power of the treasure house within you is very essential. So, what exactly is the treasure house within you? At its core, the treasure house within you is your inner self and having the right mindset. It is the place where your deepest desires, aspirations, and values reside. It is the part of you that knows what you truly want and what you are capable of achieving.

Unfortunately, for many people, the door to the treasure house within them remains locked and hidden, inaccessible to their conscious minds. To unlock the treasure house within you, you must first start by understanding yourself. This means taking the time to reflect on your life, your financial experiences, and your goals. It means being honest with yourself about what you truly want and what is holding you back. It means identifying your strengths and weaknesses, your passions and interests, and the values that guide your life. Take a look at the list below and see if you identify with any of these values and goals:

- Faith
- Family
- Freedom
- Philanthropy
- Learning
- Security
- Purpose
- Achievement
- Legacy
- Health
- Opportunities

Would you agree that in order to actualize some of these, you need to be financially stable? Once you have a clear understanding of yourself, your values, and your goals, you can begin to tap into the power of the treasure house within you. This can be done through a variety of practices, including meditation, journaling, visualization, and affirmations.

The key is to find the practices that work best for you and make them a regular part of your routine. Meditation is one of the most powerful tools for accessing the treasure house within you. By quieting your mind and focusing on your breath, you can tune out the distractions of the outside world and connect with your inner self. This can help you gain clarity, reduce stress, and tap into your inner wisdom. Hoarding money, being detached from it, overspending or even feeling guilt when you spend money on yourself are all signs that you could be imbalanced emotionally.

Journaling is another powerful tool for unlocking the treasure house within you. By writing down your thoughts and feelings, you can gain insights into your inner world and identify patterns and themes that may be holding you back. You can also use journaling to explore your values, set goals, track your progress, and celebrate your successes. Add monetary amounts to these values and goals that way you know how much to invest into the life you want to experience.

Visualization is a powerful tool for harnessing the power of the treasure house within you. By visualizing yourself achieving your goals and living the life you desire, you can tap into the power of your imagination and create a compelling vision for your future. This can help motivate you, inspire you, and keep you focused on your goals.

Affirmations are another powerful tool for accessing the treasure house within you. By repeating positive statements to yourself, you can reprogram your subconscious mind and change your beliefs and attitudes. This can help you overcome limiting beliefs, even those related to money such as "I am not good with money", "money doesn't buy happiness", "saving money is hard", "money is the root of all evil". Begin to speak the exact opposite of those negative beliefs. It may feel weird at first because we have been programmed to believe and say non-affirming things about ourselves. Make this very personal and keep at it!

The key to unlocking the treasure house within you is **consistency**. You must make a commitment to yourself to regularly practice the techniques that work best for you. This may require some discipline and effort, but the rewards are well worth it. By tapping into your inner potential and wisdom, you can achieve things you never thought possible and create a life that is fulfilling, meaningful and enjoyable.

One of the greatest benefits of accessing the treasure house within you is the sense of empowerment it brings. When you realize that you have the power within you to create the life you desire, you become less dependent on external factors for your happiness and fulfillment. You begin to trust yourself more and rely less on others for validation. You will have the confidence to even make decisions without second-guessing yourself. Take small steps towards your goals, and remember that progress is more important than perfection.

I would love to connect with you on social media, so follow me on Instagram at @otistarwoe. Check out my new book called, "The Escape Route from Poverty: Empowering Your Journey to Financial Freedom", in the back of this book's Author's Directory. And if you would like to take a trip to Kigali, Rwanda in June 2024 to attend, speak or sponsor our 2nd annual EmergHer International Business and Leadership Conference send me an email at otisttarwoe@gmail.com

GROWTH PILLAR

Chapter Six:
"They Would Have Killed Me For It"

"Building generational wealth is like creating a regenerative farm; rather than pillaging for a season, your family will harvest security and nourishment for years to come."

MARK MOLLON, CHFEBC^{SM}

CO-FOUNDER OF LEGACY BUILDER GROUP, FINANCIAL COACH, INVESTMENT ADVISOR REPRESENTATIVE

Legacy
Builder
group

As a 4th generation business owner, Mark Mollon has a passion for both entrepreneurship and educating individuals with the knowledge to create a legacy of financial security from one generation to the next. Mark is the co-founder of Legacy Builder Group, LLC. and is a licensed insurance professional and an Investment Advisor Representative with CSP Financial Group, LLC. a Registered Investment Advisor firm specializing in wealth preservation, asset protection, retirement planning, tax diversification strategies and legacy planning.

Mark spends much of his time speaking on the importance of investor awareness, covering topics such as, **"How to Defeat Your Inner Money Demons"** and **"Discovering Your True Purpose for Your Money"**. His unique areas of expertise give him an in-depth understanding of the mistakes individuals make in their financial planning.

"Money is the root of all evil" is surely a quote you've heard before. You may even know that it comes from the New Testament of the Bible.

In fact, clever as you are, many of you already know that this Scripture is misquoted as much as it's properly referenced. In my experience, this verse is potentially wielded improperly more than it's taken in its original context. Most often people leverage it to perpetuate limiting beliefs, or what I often call "money demons."

If you look up First Timothy 6:10 then you will find that the Scripture states that "the ***love*** of money is the root of all evil" *[ital. added]*.

As a Financial Advisor for over a decade, I've seen my fair share of money mismanagement, emotional-based financial decisions gone awry, and limiting financial biases that destroy financial wealth. But to this day, there is one experience that shook me to my core above all others.

The story I'm about to tell you is a perfect example of how families can be torn apart when they are focused on consuming money versus building generational wealth. Building generational wealth is like creating a regenerative farm; rather than pillaging for a season, your family will harvest security and nourishment for years to come. Sadly, my clients "Mr. and Mrs. Smith," (names have been changed), didn't grasp what it means to build a legacy through generational wealth.

Let's say you received a legitimate notice stating that you will receive $500,000,000 tax-free. How would half a billion dollars change your life today? Right now, make a list:

What Would You Do...

WITH $500,000,000?

Make a list of Ten Things you'd purchase or invest in
with an unexpected half a billion dollars.

1 _____

2 _____

3 _____

4 _____

5 _____

6 _____

7 _____

8 _____

9 _____

10 _____

We are going to come back to your list from the previous page in a moment. For now, let's learn more about the Smith Family. Mr. and Mrs. Smith have two young adult daughters. They're a warm family with a beautiful home. They live a comfortable lifestyle, earning over six figures annually. Mrs. Smith is the Matriarch of the family; she's loved and respected by everyone. Mrs. Smith has a giving spirit and is the go-to person for financial support and guidance by members of both her nuclear family as well as her community.

Mrs. Smith was savvy indeed; she wanted to make sure her financial house was in order so that at some point in her successful career, she could retire and continue to live the life that she loves with her friends and family. This is where my partner and I enter the story.

We met Mrs. Smith just before an unfortunate incident at work that affected her health. Due to the nature of the incident and the ongoing health issue Mrs. Smith would endure, she learned that she could potentially receive significant monetary compensation.

Remember my previous question about receiving $500,000,000? **That** is the monetary compensation Mrs. Smith could have received that would make her a multimillionaire, many times over… overnight. My partner and I met with the entire Smith family so that we could begin the process of creating a financial plan with the funds we anticipated. In that plan we included the daughters and the Smiths. We also included grandparents, cousins, siblings, and other men and women close to Mrs. Smith. Her family was supportive. Everybody seemed congenial, compassionate, and cooperative in creating a brighter financial future through Mrs. Smith's surprising settlement.

I recall hearing the daughters and several family members talking about what they wanted to do with their portions of the money. How would they spend it? These plans often included large purchases and travel.

As I listened to the chatter, the phrase, "my portion of the money," didn't sit right with me. Being a coach on aligning purpose with financial planning, I reflected upon how commonly people make financial decisions from an emotional state. Your feelings are impacted by temporary current environments and emotional states. Have you ever made a decision when you're excited, scared, concerned or even angry? Think of all the text messages you deleted before sending.

Wait, you delete those ones, right?!

Alas, it's human to see the temptation; the private jet rides or luxurious Parisian vacations. That doesn't mean we give into those temptations without weighing them against a long term sustainable plan. It's the reason most families with generational wealth have financial advisors with detailed rules about investing and spending money or trust funds before heirs destroy what may have been generations in the making. Perhaps it's why people like Warren Buffet are renowned for saying that he won't allow his children to inherit a huge lump sum of money; that he'll ensure they always have a need to work for what they have. Stick in the mud? Perhaps. But this story gets weirder…

Let's take a moment and revisit the $500,000,000 question next to your own list.

Was one of the top five expenses you visualized having a financial coach? *Remember, a financial advisor may not be a financial coach.*

What about discovering your true purpose for money, that which is greater than money itself?

What about discovering your Core Values?

For most people, none of the items I listed are on their lists. I trust there are some wise purchases on your list; just like Mrs. Smith and her family wisely chose to plan their future and the future of their loved ones, with my partner and me. In fact, Mrs. Smith's top concern on her list was taking care of her family.

However, people often confuse "taking care of my family" with Legacy. These aren't the same thing. Taking care of my family isn't handing out money. Truly taking care of your family is to create Multi-Generational Wealth. My business partner and I were looking forward to having Mrs. Smith and her family become educated about money and enjoy financial planning.

One night however, Mrs. Smith became gravely ill and was rushed to the hospital. When we received the call from Mr. Smith, we rushed over and were greeted by Mrs. Smith's siblings and her daughters. It was shortly after we arrived that we received the news that Mrs. Smith was on life support. We saw her the day before, smiling and full of life. We could not believe things had turned for the worse so fast. My heart broke with that family.

We headed home and that evening, I received a call from two of Mrs. Smith's siblings, requesting I provide them with all of Mrs. Smith's financial documents. I thought it was odd the siblings were asking me rather than Mr. Smith. I explained to them that financial information is confidential. There's no way I could share it in the same way I couldn't call their banker and request their personal bank statements. I explained that no family member other than Mr. Smith had Power of Attorney. Mrs. Smith did not explicitly provide permission to anybody besides Mr. Smith to handle financial matters on her behalf.

The siblings weren't pleased with my answer, although it's standard procedure in the financial industry. We ended the call and I continued with my evening. Throughout the night I wondered, "why are they requesting information? Are they not communicating with Mr. Smith?"

Later that night we got a call from Mr. Smith. I could tell he was trying very hard to keep his composure. He begged us to rush to the hospital immediately. We stopped everything and drove over.

As we were walking down the hospital hallway we were surprised to see a handful of Mrs. Smith's family members several meters away. They began walking towards us. I recall immediately seeing their posture, body language and faces and getting a negative feeling. Suddenly a family member started yelling at my business partner and me aggressively. I tried to diffuse the hostility by asking questions, but more family members joined in the tongue lashing. Suddenly, I was aware that an angry individual had turned into a mob; and the momentum was heating up enough that I feared for my partner and my safety.

Mr. Smith approached, attempting to defend us by telling the family that he had asked my partner and I to be there. Nobody listened. In fact, the situation escalated. One of the family members attacked Mr. Smith, trying to get to my female business partner and myself. Mr. Smith held the attacker off, which allowed my partner and I to escape to a nearby room with the guidance of a nurse on staff.

I was in shock not knowing what to expect next. Moments later another hospital staffer approached us with a face in disguise. We were asked to leave the premises immediately. They threatened to have us arrested if we did not comply. In fact, the police were already on their way. This was the request of the family. The same family that welcomed us with open arms…

How did things go so wrong? *Let's examine.*

Let's start with the $500,000,000 as this was the catalyst but not the source.

Money is an amplifier. If you are someone who enjoys helping people and you receive a lump sum of money, you will most likely direct quite a bit of those funds towards helping people. If you are someone who enjoys spending money on clothes, cars, shoes, etc., you will direct money to have more clothes, cars and shoes. This is common because we tend to focus on money, not wealth. Instead, we should be focused on our Values. This is why it is so important to have a Financial Coach.

As a Financial Coach, I help my clients understand the formula, "Value > Money". **Your Core Values are greater than Money.**

Discovering your values will help you focus on what guides your financial decisions. It is the glue that binds your money, family and Legacy together.

When my grandfather passed away, he left several commercial properties to eleven sons. Do you know the number of infighting over the properties? **<u>Zero</u>**.

You may think a trust would stop the fighting over inheritance. But no, all too often even a well-written trust won't stop families from trying to get their hands on more slices of the pie. I observe this on television and online as well as in the flesh at my office.

Parents steal from children, sisters and brothers isolate and abandon one another, usually forever. Families feuding over assets is a surefire way to rip apart the tapestry of decades of community and support. What's most sad in this scenario is how many beautiful souls die alone because of family infighting over money after having been estranged.

That was not the case with my uncles. Every one of my grandfather's sons understood the family Core Values. For instance, love was one of the Core Values that guided every decision. Especially during highly emotional situations, Core Values are essential for keeping your focus not on the assets (cash, cars, houses, etc.), but on what matters most to you and your family.

This is why we teach our children not to lie and steal. When push comes to shove, a child with strong Core Values won't give in to temptation or peer pressure. As adults, the temptation may not be to lie about homework to a teacher, but to destroy entire families through lying about bigger things such as money, addiction, or even fidelity.

I was too young to remember my grandfather's passing, but growing up I was happy to see how all eleven of my uncles put the well-being of our family first. Their Values directed their financial decisions and goals. This was the complete opposite for the Smiths. They focused on obtaining and consuming money, and it guided their decisions.

So how can you build a Multi-Generational Legacy? First, you need to work with a Financial Coach and Advisor. Our coaching provides clients with the structure to create a Legacy based on a person's Core Values. From there we can build the financial and estate plan that aligns with the goals for you, your family and generations to come.

That is how you allow others to experience your existence, your Legacy, for generations to come.

Disclosures:
Information in this publication does not involve the rendering of personalized investment, insurance, tax nor legal advice but is limited to the dissemination of general educational information on financial instruments, products or services. None of the content should be viewed as an offer to buy or sell, or as a solicitation of an offer to buy or sell any of the securities discussed. A licensed, qualified, investment, insurance, tax or legal professional advisor should always be consulted before implementing any of the options presented.

Chapter Seven:

"Unlocking Financial Clarity and Growth: Strategies for Business Owners"

ROBIN R. HAYNES, MBA, RFC®

Business Advisor, Financial Strategist

Robin R. Haynes, is a seasoned professional in the financial industry with more than 20 years of experience. Robin is committed and passionate about teaching the basics of finances and entrepreneurship, making sure there is a thorough understanding of the financial behaviors and habits necessary for success.

Along with her work as a financial strategist for small businesses, Robin is a business advisor for the Goldman Sachs 10,000 Small Business Program in Baltimore. Robin holds a B.S. in Accounting, and a M.B.A. in Entrepreneurial Studies. Robin also holds a Registered Financial Consultant ® Designation from The International Association of Registered Financial Consultants (IARFC). Robin's literary work include: "The Fundamentals Of Finances Applied To Everyday Living" and "This Is Not The Final Chapter."

In the dynamic yet complex landscape of business, entrepreneurs face a myriad of challenges as they navigate their journey. One common hurdle that entrepreneurs oftentimes have to overcome is not having a complete understanding regarding the functionality of their financial picture. This knowledge gap often leads to the unhealthy financial decisions that prevent a business from growing.

Within this chapter, we will provide strategies for understanding the flow of money within your business, provide strategies for business growth as well as assist you in understanding external capital - the need, how it will be disbursed and your ability to repay.

Many entrepreneurs find themselves having a difficult time with various internal components due to a lack of financial clarity within their business. As a business advisor, I often notice how business owners "shy" away from talking about their business financial picture. I'm often told, "I let my accountant handle all things financial when it comes to my business".

Understanding your financial picture and how the finances work within your business isn't that hard - I PROMISE YOU! Honestly you have to take your time to learn, study and ask key questions. If you don't know what questions to ask, connect with individuals who can assist you with understanding as well as, guide you through your financial space until you become comfortable.

Strategies for Understanding The Flow of Money Within Your Business

In the entrepreneurial space there are many economic complexities and uncertainties. It is imperative that you understand and equip yourself with the necessary tools and strategies to understand your business financial picture. Only through this understanding can you position yourself for sustainability and growth.

To gain a comprehensive understanding of your financial picture, as an entrepreneur I strongly recommend that you focus on the continuation of educating yourself on the financial mechanics as well as implement effective money management practices. This involves:

a) **Implementing and Maintaining Accurate Bookkeeping:** Maintaining up-to-date and accurate financial records enables you to track revenue, expenses, and cash flow. This provides a clear picture of your business's financial health and assists you in making informed business decisions.

b) **Financial Statements Analysis:** Regularly reviewing financial statements, such as your balance sheets, income statements, and cash flow statements, provides a deeper insight into your business's profitability and liquidity. This analysis helps identify areas for improvement and informs strategic decision-making.

c) **Budgeting and Forecasting:** Creating realistic budgets and financial forecasts allows you to plan for future expenses, manage cash flow effectively, and anticipate potential financial challenges. Budgeting and forecasting also provides a framework to make informed business decisions.

Strategies for Business Growth

Business growth can be exciting and scary at the same time. When it comes to business growth, there are a few ways that you can grow and or expand. Growth and expansion can include the following:

1. Expanding to New Demographics or Geographies
2. Expanding your business to new demographics or geographies presents opportunities for revenue growth. To successfully execute this strategy, you as the business owner should consider the following:

   a) **Market Research:** Thoroughly researching the target demographic or geography helps identify potential demand, competition, and market trends. Understanding your customer needs and preferences is crucial for tailoring products or services effectively. Market research will inform your client that you are in alignment with their needs

b) **Strategic Partnerships:** Collaborating with other local businesses or establishing strategic partnerships in the target market can provide access to a larger customer base, as well as distribution networks. These alliances can accelerate growth and mitigate risks associated with entering a new market.

c) **Marketing and Promotion:** Developing targeted marketing campaigns and employing effective promotional strategies tailored to your new demographic or geography increases brand visibility and attracts potential customers. Understanding and leveraging digital marketing techniques can also maximize your customer reach and engagement.

Introducing New Products or Services to Existing Demographics

Diversifying product or service offerings can fuel revenue growth and deepen your customer relationships. To successfully introduce new products or services, I recommend you to consider the following:

a) **Customer Feedback and Research:** Gathering feedback from existing customers and conducting market research helps identify gaps in the market and potential areas for expansion. Obtaining customer feedback should also be used as a training tool, which will allow you and your team to strengthen those areas that are frail. Understanding your customers' pains/issues allows for you to be innovative with creating solutions that addresses your customers needs.

b) **Product and Service Development:** Introducing a new product or service, takes time, patience and strategy. Before you launch a new product or service I strongly suggest that you:

i. Understand its purpose, don't launch a new product or service because it sounds nice. Be sure that the new product or service will be sustainable both now and in your business future.

ii. Develop a detailed plan outlining the product/service features, benefits, and unique selling points. This will serve as a roadmap for your development process and ensure that you stay focused on the core objectives.

iii. Create prototypes or samples of the product/service to test and gather feedback from existing and potential customers. This will allow you to make necessary improvements and refine your offering before your official launch.

iv. Establish a pricing strategy that aligns with the value provided by your new product/service. Consider factors such as production costs, competition, and perceived value to determine the optimal pricing structure.

v. Build a strong marketing and promotional campaign to create awareness and generate excitement about your new offering. Utilize various channels such as social media (know what platform your target market uses the most and penetrate that particular platform), and advertising, to reach your target audience effectively.

vi. Train your team members on the features, benefits, and usage of the new product/service. Ensure they are well-equipped to handle customer inquiries and provide exceptional support.

vii. Conduct a soft launch or beta testing phase to gain initial customer feedback and identify any potential issues or areas for improvement. This will allow you to make necessary adjustments before you fully launch.

viii. Monitor the market response and collect data on sales, customer feedback, and satisfaction levels. Continuously analyze this information to make informed decisions and refine your product/service offering over time.

ix. Lastly, be prepared to adapt and evolve your product/service based on changing market trends and customer demands. Regularly evaluate the performance and relevance of your offering to ensure its long-term success.

Remember, launching a new product or service is a dynamic process that requires ongoing evaluation, adjustment, and customer-centric approach to ensure its sustainability and success within the market.

Understanding External Capital: The Need, Disbursement, and Payback

Now that we've discussed a few strategies for growth, let's take a deeper dive as to how you're going to obtain external capital to facilitate your growth.

As an entrepreneur, the need for capital is a common necessity for growth, expansion, and or possibly unforeseen financial mishaps. While internal funding sources like retained earnings or reinvesting profits are often the first choice, there are and will be situations where obtaining external capital become vital. In this part of the chapter we will take a closer look at the reasoning behind needing external capital, the disbursement process, and the importance of assessing your repayment ability.

Why External Capital?
External capital plays a crucial role in meeting various business goals and objectives. External funding will also provide necessary resources for you to facilitate your growth opportunities in a timely manner.

How Will You Disburse The Capital?
Once you've made the decision to seek external capital, understanding the disbursement process is crucial. Key considerations for disbursement include:

1. **Funding Sources:** External capital can be obtained from various sources such as financial institutions (banks or credit unions), venture capitalists, angel investors, private equity firms, or crowdfunding platforms. Each funding source has its own requirements, terms, and conditions, which must be thoroughly evaluated before proceeding.

2. **Doing Your Due Diligence:** Potential investors or lenders will conduct their due diligence as it pertains to assessing the viability of your business. It's up to you as the entrepreneur/business owner to have a complete understanding as to how the requested capital will be used. As you are in communication with the potential funding source, you want to be in position to address "how the money will be used". Remember: being prepared with comprehensive and accurate information is essential for securing external capital.

Your Financial Position and Ability To Repay
Before seeking external capital, it is critical to evaluate your financial position and repayment ability. Examine the following factors:

1. **Debt Capacity:** Assess your existing debt and determine if you are in a financial position to acquire additional debt at this time. (REMEMBER timing and strategy are extremely important)

2. **Revenue and Profitability:** Evaluate your revenue streams and profitability to determine your ability to generate sufficient cash flow for repayment. External factors such as market demand, competition, and potential risks could impact your ability to meet repayment obligations.

3. **Repayment Strategy:** Develop a clear plan for repayment. This may include a combination of strategies such as, implementing cost-saving measures, or generating additional revenue streams. Having a well-thought-out repayment strategy demonstrates your commitment to honoring your financial obligations.

Obtaining external capital can be a viable solution for businesses in need of funding. However, it is crucial to carefully consider the reasons behind needing capital, understand the disbursement process, and assess your financial position and repayment ability. Thoroughly evaluating these factors, will assist you in making sound decisions that align with your business goals and financial capabilities.

Chapter Eight:

"The Winning Team"

LYNDSAÉ PEELE, MBA, PMEC™

Chief Wealth Officer

Lyndsae Peele, MBA, PMECTM is a results-driven finance coach, international speaker, and black wealth advocate. She received her BA in Broadcast Journalism from Howard University, her MBA from the University of Maryland Global Campus, and her certification in Women's Entrepreneurship at Cornell University. Lyndsae was recently appointed as the new Kiva US Entrepreneurial Ecosystem Manager. She supports a portfolio of 35+ community-based Kiva lending partners (called Hubs) and their 40+ staff members (called Capital Access Managers) across the US and Puerto Rico. They aim to expand access to capital and drive financial inclusion with non-traditional, no-fee, no-interest, crowdfunded financing in their communities. She is also the Chief Wealth Officer of the award-winning financial services company, Kingdom Vision Consulting. Lyndsae' combined her years of banking experience and her passion for economic development, to create a socially conscious organization specializing in personal and business finance for entrepreneurs of color. Kingdom Vision has been honored as the SBA's 2022 Maryland Financial Services Champion of the Year.

In a recent interview, Rick Ross said "You have to be mindful of what you think because you will always listen to yourself." If you tell yourself that you can't start that business, you just may never start that business. If you tell yourself that it will be impossible to make over 6-figures doing what you love, you will discount your ability to charge your worth. If you tell yourself that you cannot trust anyone to support you with your finances, you will never ask for help. In almost every area of our lives, it takes a group of people to collectively work together to accomplish a shared goal. In church, we have a pastor who takes the primary lead, however, we have deacons, missionaries, mothers, and other leaders who carry the church on their shoulders.

When it comes to our health, we have a team that we rarely select on our own to provide for us. We have physicians, nurses, lab techs, billing specialists, and other roles that we don't often engage with. We also have dentists, chiropractors, nurse practitioners, and whomever else we may need to assist us with your physical needs. Some of these roles may provide similar services but they all still have their own processes and distinctive purpose for the work they do to support us.

Even when we think about our mental health team, we have therapists, psychologists, counselors, reiki practitioners, and other providers who address our specific needs that they specialize in.

Growing up we were often reminded that, "It takes a village to raise a child". There was an unspoken connection and responsibility among neighborhoods, community organizers, and families. We knew that if something happened to one of our children, it happened to all of our children.

Along the way, we saw that this posture was only applicable to those topics that we were comfortable with as a community. When faced with topics that were more uncomfortable, we shrunk as a connected body and were forced to face certain challenges alone including our financial health.

While it takes a village to raise a child, it also takes a village to create, maintain, and preserve your wealth. Identifying financial partners that resonate with your core values, future goals, and current capacity can produce a wealth of knowledge, income opportunities, and social capital, your teams' network now becomes your extended network.

We have to understand that the people we bring into our financial family to help us with our money are just as important as the team that takes care of our health. The difference is that you can personally choose everyone who supports your financial growth versus your health team being assigned to you.

This allows you the freedom and flexibility to choose who you work with and how you work with them. This is an opportunity to build connections and relationships that transform who you are financially and who your family can become.

The Winning Wealth Team

Creating relationships with financial partners that you align with will propel you to accelerate your growth, strengthen your accountability, and increase your tangible and intangible assets. There's an old African proverb that says "If you want to go quickly, go alone. If you want to go far, go together." If we apply this to our mindset around building a winning wealth team, we set ourselves up to achieve our wildest financial dreams while expanding our knowledge beyond our own perspectives and experiences.

The first step to identifying who you need on your team is to understand where you currently stand financially. Ask yourself these questions:

- What are my short & long-term goals?
- What are my challenges and external barriers?
- What area of my finances needs the most support right now?
- Who do I need to connect with first to gain access to the other resource partners?

Answering these questions gives you a starting point for building your winning team. Once you know where you are and where you are going, it's important to take an assessment of who you already have in your network. Even if you do not connect with them often, normally we have at least one financial professional that we know, have seen, or have been introduced to at some point.

While there is a long list of financial professions that we need in our community, it is important to start with your core group of people and build upon that foundation. Typically, we recommend starting with your B.A.I.L team. Your B.A.I.L team consists of your Business Banker,

Accountant, Insurance Agent, and Lawyer. Prior to arranging your initial individual meetings that will progress into group sessions, you must understand each person's role and how you may be

able to leverage their skillset.

Let's start with your banker. Your banking partner will be your biggest advocate, referral partner, and cheerleader. During my time as a personal and business banker, I felt that it was my duty to make sure that my clients were exposed to any and every opportunity that came across my desk, especially when they sacrificed their time to build sustainable relationships with me. There is power in proximity and it is important to know that bankers are usually a core component of the wealth team.

Your banker will make sure that you are aware of the internal and external resources that can benefit you, your family, and even your business. While most banks have the same or similar products, sometimes it's the position of your banker that can make those products and services worth your while. During my time as a business banker, I had a client who was interested in applying for a line of credit to grow her business. She had previously been declined from her primary institution and a few others. I was able to build a foundation of trust with my client that went both ways, from her to me and from me to her. Fast forward to the initial application submission, we applied and were declined due to credit challenges. However, because she was a client whom I had taken the opportunity to know and build a relationship with, I made a few calls to our underwriting team. After advocating for her and her business, we were able to get the decision overturned. It was a gentle reminder that relationships are the most valuable asset in your life, and especially your finances.

In addition to internal benefits, your banker presents a number of external benefits to you as well. A good banker will typically be ingrained in the community and have access to various community networks such as chambers of commerce, women's business centers, technical assistance providers, alternative lenders, various centers of influence, and other local resources. Your next financial partner, cohort program, board member, or funding opportunity may come as a recommendation from your banker.

Your next B.A.I.L. partner is your accountant. It is imperative that you have a great accountant that does more than just file your tax returns. Building a valuable relationship with your accountant should include year-round tax planning, annual personal and accompanying returns, the filing of your annual report if you're in business, and even bookkeeping if that is a service that is offered. Your accountant is one of the most important players on your team because they determine how the financial vehicles that your other partners bring to the table get delivered to the IRS. Your accountant can stand between you paying most of your income in taxes or being able to shelter some of that income to take care of your family. While we love that accountants are great at reducing our taxable income, it is relevant that they also understand your short-term lending goals so that their service to you does not become a barrier with your lender. As soon as you have a banker and an accountant, you should make an introduction to each other as they will probably work together the most.

Your insurance agent is another key partner in your finances to take care of the what-ifs of today and the inevitable passings of tomorrow. You want to connect with your insurance agent at least once a year to review your policies whether they are for living benefits, after-death benefits, or a combination of both. Your agent will make sure that you have the proper coverage to supplement your income, cover your final expenses, and cover any burial expenses. As you deepen your relationship with your agent, you also allow room for them to offer additional or reduced coverage for all of your other needs as well. Each year during your review, make sure you are also updating any beneficiaries just in case things have changed within your family.

Your lawyer may not be someone you speak to every month or even every quarter, however, you want to have someone that you can call or email when you need them. The idea is to choose a lawyer that can support you in various legal matters from estate planning to business. When estate planning, you want to make sure you have a will, maybe a trust fund, a power of attorney if you become incapacitated, and other important documents that can protect you and your family. Having a lawyer in your ecosystem ensures that you can remain compliant and legally protected.

Once we have a core team that has built rapport and proven themselves as reliable, we are ready to add a few other financial partners to your wealth team. A few people to consider adding to your wealth team would be:

- A Coach - whether you are a business owner, committed employee, or somewhere in between, having a coach will always be a great addition. Your coach will help to provide an outside opinion that provides unbiased recommendations and guidance while also providing accountability. Your financial coach may also act as a centerpiece for every other partner and act as a bridge in forming those relationships.
- A Financial Advisor - no matter how much money you have to invest right now, having a financial advisor who can help you connect the dots between your goals and your reality is always a bonus. Your advisor will help you understand and

articulate your retirement goals, your risk tolerance, and your ideal portfolio makeup. Everyone does not desire to invest or plan for retirement the same and that's okay. However, having a licensed professional will help you to identify the particular method that leads you to accomplish your goals. It is important to have an advisor who can provide expertise or connect you with resources from multiple investment sources from the stock market to real estate, franchising, angel investing, and anything else that you may want to add to your portfolio.

- A Bookkeeper - while some accountants are bookkeepers or offer that service, some do not. If your accountant does not, it's okay, you just have to find a third party to provide that service. If you are in business, monthly reconciliation of your books is extremely important. This allows you to see the trends in your business while giving you access to financial reports that everyone else on your wealth team may need to see at some point in your journey.

- A CDFI partner- a CDFI is a Community Development Financial Institution that provides capital, technical assistance, and educational seminars for entrepreneurs who may be credit-challenged or credit-invisible. I always recommend that no matter what stage of business you are in, you should seek a CDFI partner to be in proximity to the resources being shared by local, state, and federal government. These nonprofits are federally designated and usually funded by the government and corporations. Most CDFIs are SBA lenders and can support you from the ideation stage of your business to succession planning.

While there are a few other financial professionals that you may benefit from, we want you to start with your core team and strategically grow over time. The more you meet with your team and see your goals being checked off of your list, the more confident you will become in being the CEO of your finances and leading your winning wealth team.

Contact Information

Personal Brand

- IG: @mywealthconnector
- Website: www.mywealthconnector.com

Business

- IG, Facebook, LinkedIn: @kingdomvisionconsult @collectivechats
- Website: www.kingdomvisionconsult.com www.thekingdomwealthcollective.com

Chapter Nine:

"Double Taxation Doesn't Scare Me"

TEDDY "THE TAX MAN" PRIOLEAU, EA

Enrolled Agent

Teddy Prioleau – widely known as Teddy The Tax Man – is an Enrolled Agent, who has been in practice for over a third of a century. He has a weekly segment on the morning news in Baltimore where he offers tax advice to a one million household viewing audience. Also, he can be heard every Thursday evening on wclmradionline.com, where he discusses topics such as retirements, taxes and other financial information that is important to households at all levels of the income spectrum. Teddy is also interviewed on a regular basis on the historic Howard University Radio (WHUR) and many other radio stations around the country. He is past chairman of the board of a 12,000 member credit union, where he still actively serves on the board. He is a past chairman of the membership committee of the Maryland Society of Accountants, and continues to serve on other boards that gladly use his talents to further their advancement in their areas of service.

After preparing 18,000 tax returns in a 30 year span, Teddy sold his tax practice and expanded his retirements and investments practice, to focus on the long-term financial health of clients all over the nation.

As of this writing, I'm in my forty-third year of being a tax professional. *Forty-third!* Did I have ANY idea at all that I'd ever have the opportunity to say that? Absolutely not! I'm always being asked, "How did you end up in the tax profession, and where did the pseudonym Teddy the Tax Man™ come from?"

I'm certain that those who asked, are looking for a tear jerking, moving, heartfelt story from me, but it's as simple as this: my father dabbled in taxes when I was a child. He only prepared returns for relatives, close friends and coworkers. His office was our dining room table. After he completed tax returns, clients would hand him over cash money. Greenbacks. Ducats. I saw all that, and I wanted it. That's it! No fancy story. Nothing to write home about. But if you'd like to make a movie of it, just let me know.

How did the name Teddy The Tax Man come about? It was one day in the early nineties, a couple minutes after 06:00 a.m. Eastern Time, and I was up preparing to go to work. I was listening to the radio, when one of the listeners called in with some issues that she was having. She was describing why the day before was a really bad day. One of those reasons happened to be the fact that her babysitter - that's what they were called before the advent of the term 'daycare provider' came about - would not give her social security number to this lady who called in to the radio show. The caller wanted to claim the credit on her tax return. I called the hotline, the number that no outsider was supposed to have, well, except for me and the many girlfriends of one of the DJs. I explained to the DJ, who was a friend of mine, that he should announce over the radio, that all that lady had to do was to write the word 'unable' on the child care form, and the Internal Revenue Service would honor that.

"Maaaan, do you think I'm going to remember that? I'll tell you what. Let me record you giving that answer, and I will play it at the next break. How about that?" After he played it on the radio, he closed it out by saying, "That was Teddy The Tax Man!" That's where the legend began.

A Surprising Tax Tip That Will Blow Your Hair Back!
"I recommend your entity be structured as a C-Corporation, so that you can save on taxes," is not something you'll hear come out of the mouth of a tax professional… ever. That is, until something called the Tax Cut & Jobs Act or TCJA. TCJA is a major piece of tax legislation that President Trump signed into law on December 22, 2017. TCJA was the most significant overhaul of the US tax code in several decades, and many of its statutes affect you and your businesses today. In this section, I'll give you one example of how TCJA transformed my business and the tax burdens of many of my clients.

TCJA was designed to simplify the tax code *(very funny…),* lower tax rates for individuals and businesses, and stimulate economic growth. Among other things, here are some of the key changes brought about by TCJA that may impact you or your business.

1. Individual Tax Rates and Deductions

The TCJA adjusted the tax brackets and rates for individual taxpayers, generally reducing tax rates for most income levels. The standard deduction was significantly increased, providing a larger deduction for those who do not itemize their deductions.

2. Child Tax Credit

The Child Tax Credit was increased from $1,000 to $2,000 per qualifying child, and the income thresholds for eligibility were raised.

3. State and Local Tax Deductions

There were changes to the deduction for state and local taxes (SALT), limiting the amount that can be deducted to $10,000.

4. Corporate Tax Rate

The corporate tax rate was reduced from a maximum of 35% to a flat rate of 21%.

5. Pass-Through Businesses

Certain pass-through businesses, such as sole proprietorships, partnerships, and S corporations, received a deduction of up to 20% of qualified business income.

6. Estate Tax

The estate tax exemption amount was doubled, reducing the number of estates subject to the estate tax.

7. Alternative Minimum Tax (AMT)

The AMT was retained but with higher exemption amounts, resulting in fewer individuals being subject to this tax.

8. Repatriation of Overseas Profits

The TCJA introduced a one-time tax on the repatriation of overseas profits held by U.S. corporations.

9. Healthcare Individual Mandate

The TCJA eliminated the penalty for individuals who do not maintain health insurance coverage, effectively repealing the individual mandate of the Affordable Care Act.

In the next few moments, I'll dive into one of the many changes that TCJA had on my practice, and that's the issue of "double taxation." Over the past forty-three years I've worked as an Enrolled Agent. Thirteen years ago I sold my tax practice after preparing 18,000 tax returns so that I could focus on the long-term financial health of clients. One of the "boogeymen" in my business has been this double taxation factor, but in this chapter I'll show you why you don't need to be scared of it any longer.

Since I began my practice in the 1980's, the tax rates for C-Corporations have always been high. The issue of "double taxation" occurs when a C-Corporation pays its shareholders a dividend, but the shareholders as well as the C-Corp pay taxes on the same money. It's IRS double dipping!

How does this happen? First, the C-Corporation is not permitted to deduct that dividend as an expense, which means the C-Corp will pay taxes on that money, even though the Corporation no longer has that money. Then the shareholder will pay taxes on the same dividend. This creates what we have referred to as "double taxation" already in this chapter. It's exactly what it sounds like: money being taxed twice.

In 2017 when The Tax Cut & Jobs Act came into effect, America hopefully held its breath awaiting deep tax cuts on the individual level. For decades we've suspected that the folks behind the curtain, so to speak, were going to shake things up on the business tax side, after all. That shakeup came in the form of reducing the C-Corporation tax rate from 35% all the way down to 21%. And no, that's not a typo. I didn't stutter, although I almost choked on my tongue when I read this.

Put down your coffee and remove the chewing gum from your mouth for this next one... As of 2022, the C-Corporation rates are lower than five of the personal tax rates. I know, this sounds crazy... but once you pick your chin up off the floor, let's move on because there's more...

So what about the issue of Double Taxation?

I'm only going to say this once: **double taxation doesn't scare me!** You see, Even if my personal tax rate is 39% and I'm the shareholder of a C-Corp, I will still only pay 21% on some of my money, by virtue of the Corporation being mine.

(Tax purists won't like the way I phrased that, but that is actually the case.)

If my entity is a single-member LLC with a net income of $539,900, **all** of my money would be taxed at the 39% rate if I'm happy, but in this scenario I'm married and the amount of taxable net income is $647,850 (chuckle).

And... the dividend distributions from my profitable Corporation will be taxed at a **maximum** 20%, no matter what my personal tax rate is.

What's more, if your LLC is profitable, you will pay taxes on that net income in that same year, whether you take distributions or not. If you do take dividend distributions from your C-Corporation, you don't pay taxes on that income until you receive those distributions.

But wait! There's more! If your SMLLC (single-member limited liability company) is profitable, you will pay taxes on that net income in THAT year, whether you take distribution or not. If you take dividend distributions from your C Corp, you don't pay taxes on that income until you receive those distributions.

Right now, someone out there in Reading Land is saying, "Teddy The Tax Man™, that 21% income tax rate sure sounds good to me. But aren't you forgeţng that the tax laws can change like THAT (snap your fingers here)." My answer is, "No. I know how fast things can change in this profession. I also know that some provisions of the TCJA (Tax Cuts and Jobs Act) are set to expire in a few years. NOT THIS ONE! The reduction of the C-Corporation tax rate is said to be 'permanent' and because of the political climate at this writing, I simply do not expect any changes in this arena.

Additionally, if your clients would have taken advantage of this tax rate immediately, they would have already enjoyed a 14% drop in their federal tax liabilities for a minimum of five years. That's BIG! Moreover, the Internal Revenue Service audits the schedule C filer a whole lot more often than it audits the C-Corporation. Now, if that doesn't impact your client's decision as to whether this entity should get some consideration, I'm not sure what will.

If you need another reason why I think that the C corporation is a viable option, I'll give it to you. Imagine the following scenario. A sole proprietor (for this example, a sole proprietor is the same as a single-member limited liability company owner) is seeking a loan from his/her lending institution. It doesn't matter whether it's business or personal. It doesn't matter whether it's a car loan, first mortgage or home equity. Since the sole proprietor doesn't receive a W-2 from his/her entity to show the lender, it is very likely that that sole proprietor will have to go through extra hoops to prove income. Those hoops could include, but are not limited to, that taxpayer having to pay extra money in order to have financial statements created. If you are the tax advisor/consultant, that's good news for you, but not great news for that taxpayer. Okay, the financials look good. Ironically, the lender needs even more information. That information is the proof that estimated taxes are paid. Compare that to the average taxpayer who DOES receive a W-2 from his/her employer. The W-2 is turned over to the lending institution, and the process begins. That ONE document reveals the borrower's income AND taxes withheld, and he/she didn't have to pay ANY person, ANY extra for ANY reports.

In case you haven't been convinced that the C-Crop is a perfectly viable option, let me offer you just a little more. When setting up and running a business, it is not unusual for the owner to need someone else who is willing to come in and be a co-owner. This is helpful because many times there is a need for talent other than the owner of the business. That co-owner could be a good financial source for the entity, and he/she could be a person who is talented enough that he or she would probably deserve to share in the profits of the corporation. Well, the entity could not be a sole proprietorship or a single-member LLC, for obvious reasons.

Since I am recommending the corporate structure, let's stay away from the multi member LLC or the partnership. At this point, you're probably thinking, okay but we still have the S-Corporation as an option. Yes, that is true. But the S-Corporation can have a maximum of 100

shareholders, and that has only increased from 75 in recent years. A C-Corporation can have an unlimited number of shareholders. Sure, I realize that the average C-Corporation which is our client, has far fewer than 100 shareholders. It's just that when I am recommending an entity structure for a client, I want that client to have as many wins as possible. To me the unlimited number of shareholders is yet another win.

Why should a client bother with any of this? We live in a litigation crazy society. Everyone wants to sue for the least little incident or situation. Generally speaking, except where fraud has been perpetrated, the C-Corporation will protect its shareholders from litigants in a case against the corporation.

That means, again, generally speaking, if a corporation loses a case, the shareholders' personal assets are not at risk. I have to use the phrase 'generally speaking,' because that's a safety net. Unfortunately, every situation and every case is based on its own merits. If sole proprietorships and partnerships offered the same protection as the C-Corporation, that would be one more reason for those two entities to even be considered. They don't, so stick with the C-Corporation.

Obviously, when we're giving clients that PAID consultation, there are other factors to consider. I'm just recommending that we don't revert to the days of yore, when our bodies were trained to go into shock at the mere mention of the word 'C corporation.'

DOUBLE TAXATION DOESN'T SCARE ME!!

Teddy The Tax Man™

Disclosures:
Information in this publication does not involve the rendering of personalized investment, insurance, tax nor legal advice but is limited to the dissemination of general educational information on financial instruments, products or services. None of the content should be viewed as an offer to buy or sell, or as a solicitation of an offer to buy or sell any of the securities discussed. A licensed, qualified, investment, insurance, tax or legal professional advisor should always be consulted before implementing any of the options presented.

Chapter Ten:
"DeFi and its Impact on the Black Community"

KAMAL R HUBBARD, JD CFE CSX

Author | Advocate | Blockchain Consultant

Kamal Hubbard is a civil rights officer who spent several years managing research at Stanford University's Rock Center for Corporate Governance. While there, he worked with a former Securities and Exchange Commissioner examining federal securities litigation and global corruption cases. Kamal is certified in Fraud Examination, Cybersecurity, and Decentralized Finance. Mr. Hubbard had the privilege of testifying before California's Senate Banking Committee and served as part of the Blockchain Advocacy Coalition. Kamal also participated in discussions with the US Department of the Treasury's Office of the Comptroller of the Currency on matters related to the intersection of cryptocurrencies and banking.

The era of digital money is upon us. During the early days of the coronavirus pandemic, shortages of cash and coins alongside other necessities became apparent. The limitations on physical currency led to a fervent search for alternative payment methods, sparking a movement to transition people away from traditional cash. Reports from South Korea indicated that paper currency was being burned to control the spread of the virus. In my mind, forcing people to use digital payments could someday mean the use of cryptocurrencies would be even more of a highly contested topic among financial institutions and governments. For this reason, it is imperative that we consider the potential impact of this shift towards digital currency.

This may be the first time some readers may have come across the concept of cryptocurrencies. For those who have, bear with me as I quickly explain how they work. Cryptocurrencies, like Bitcoin operate using an underlying technology called blockchain. Think of a blockchain like a global online hotel guest ledger, where lots of people can make entries at various locations around the world at the same time. When someone adds a new entry to the book, everyone else can see it and they all agree that other guest entries are there.

Everytime someone adds a piece of information to the book, it gets added to the existing pages that already have information. This makes it very hard for anyone to change or erase something that's already in the book, because it would be like trying to erase guest entries that have already been made. Now instead of guest entries, imagine the information were records of payments made or other data. Blockchain is incredibly helpful for things like keeping track of who owns what or who has been paid, because once something is written in the book, everyone can see it, and everyone agrees that it is true. For this reason, blockchains are regarded as highly transparent.

To underscore another aspect of blockchain technology, I would like to explain the concept of decentralization. Decentralization is a concept that means spreading out power and control so that no one person or group has too much of it. Think of a company where the owner oversees everything, from what type of work is undertaken to how the company's money is spent. That's a very centralized system - the company's owner has a lot of power and control over everything that happens. Now consider if the company was a cooperative, where all the employees owned the business who all had a say in what happened with the company. Maybe one employee oversees accounting, and another is in charge of sales, and they all work together to make decisions about the company. That is a decentralized system. Instead of one person or a group of a few making all the decisions, power and control is spread out across many different people who work together to make decisions.

Decentralization is important because it helps make sure that power and control isn't concentrated in the hands of a few. It also means that different perspectives and ideas can be considered when making decisions.

Cryptocurrencies are digital or virtual currencies that use strong encryption techniques to secure their transactions and to control the creation of new units. Unlike conventional currencies that are controlled by a central bank, cryptocurrencies use blockchain technology to keep track of all the transactions and to make sure each transaction is transparent. The other key feature of cryptocurrencies is that no one person or institution controls them, thus making them decentralized. The transparent and decentralized elements of cryptocurrencies resonate with so many people in the black community because they are very much opposed to how the traditional banking and financial systems currently work.

Despite the evidence that there is a strong number of people in the global Black family that use and believe in the promise cryptocurrencies, there are not enough of us currently that are using them in a way that would be able to improve our overall economic condition. Although Bitcoin is speculated to have tremendous upside potential, it is not a complete solution for the Black community. I say this because we have no sizable stake in the ownership of the network, no say in the decision making of the network, and no measurable control of the mining of Bitcoin. Additionally, I would be remiss if I did not mention how the blockchain and cryptocurrency industry does much to tout the benefits of how this technology can help our community but has not done nearly enough to demonstrate how that is the case or protect us from the pitfalls.

Not long after chattel slavery, the Freedman's Bank was established to accept the deposits of newly freed former slaves. As bank branches and treasuries grew, a movement to defraud the Freedwomen and Freedmen was afoot. The White trustees amended the bank's charter without warning its Black depositors, which once discovered, led to the bank's failure and loss of nearly 80 million in today's dollars. The Freedman's Bank represented a betrayal that explains why many Black people in America have a uniquely untrusting relationship with the legacy financial system. So, from the very beginning of our emancipation from slavery and ability to earn money in the United States, there have been efforts to derail financial progress in our community. Other factors, like the lack of access to capital, redlining, predatory lending in the Black community demonstrate how traditional finance has also done quite a bit to widen the Racial Wealth Gap.

The Digital Divide is the difference in access between Black and White households to broadband internet and other digital technology. This inequality plays into the already difficult learning curve associated with blockchain and cryptocurrencies. These factors combined with the Racial Wealth Gap make for an almost insurmountable obstruction for our people to adopt this game changing area of computer science in more substantial numbers. However, I know what our community has accomplished. I know what we have endured. I know what we are capable of and an understanding of these considerations makes me optimistic that if we embrace decentralized finance, we have a chance to use it to help close the Racial Wealth Gap.

Now more than ever, it is imperative that we re-examine our relationship with money. Part of my studies on the history of money taught me that some ancient forms of African currencies were regarded as having a soul. If a denomination had somehow become damaged in the course of commerce, its soul would need to be repaired or the denomination would be discarded as worthless. This reverence for money as if it were a soul instead of a means to an end is something worth keeping in mind.

Now consider decentralized finance also known as "DeFi." DeFi also operates on blockchain technology and allows for trustless and permissionless access to online platforms like decentralized exchanges, decentralized money markets, decentralized stablecoins, decentralized insurance, and decentralized derivatives. Essentially, it contains everything the existing traditional financial system has to offer, however, with DeFi we can remove the discrimination that has been present in traditional finance. DeFi has a few characteristics that give it a distinct advantage over any centralized financial system.

First, blockchain is open, meaning anyone, anywhere, at any time, across the world with an internet connected device can access it. Second, the records kept in DeFi protocols are also decentralized, so no central server or body of authority has overarching control over the entire system. Third, it is trustless, meaning that a party to a transaction does not need to trust another party for that transaction to be facilitated. Lastly, DeFi as a permissionless ecosystem, means that authorization by a third party is also not necessary for a transaction to go through. In other words, we don't need permission to use it!

The use of DeFi to boost our economy can at least remove discrimination from the equation and much of the friction and fees present in traditional finance that increases the costs of international transactions. The reality is if you live in a certain zip code, have a criminal record, work a certain type of job, own a certain type of business, or any other reason someone with authority in the traditional banking system does not feel you are worthy of credit; you will not have a loan extended to you, money or access to capital.

Decentralized finance is a powerful tool that can be used to help the black community if we choose to adopt it. By using DeFi, we can revolutionize the way Black people access capital and turn a banking system built on exclusion into an open-source, transparent platform for everyone regardless of their background. In doing so, we can alleviate some of the most oppressive forces against Black people in favor of decentralized solutions that I hope one day we can create for ourselves, for our own best interests to create a more equitable and sustainable global Black Economy.

Disclosures:
Information in this publication does not involve the rendering of personalized investment, insurance, tax nor legal advice but is limited to the dissemination of general educational information on financial instruments, products or services. None of the content should be viewed as an offer to buy or sell, or as a solicitation of an offer to buy or sell any of the securities discussed. A licensed, qualified, investment, insurance, tax or legal professional advisor should always be consulted before implementing any of the options presented.

Chapter Eleven:

"Accelerating Prosperity: Unleashing Your Entrepreneurial Financial Growth"

DR. MICHELLE S. THOMAS
Business Surgeon

Dr. Michelle S. Thomas, Your Business Surgeon is the Executive FOUNDER/ CEO of The Exceptional Woman Enterprise. An Enterprise created to remove the barriers of sustainable growth that often interrupt the potentials of success for many women entrepreneurs, especially women of color. The Exceptional Woman Enterprise consists of RESULT-DRIVEN entities focusing on providing Mastery Level tools of business principles for a clear understanding of each complex level of their entrepreneurial journey.

Dr. Michelle has leveraged her years of collective first-hand experiences with growing profitable businesses to become the reputable author, motivational speaker, and coach she is today. Whether she is public speaking, performing as a conference Keynote speaker, conducting online courses, or offering personal or professional coaching services, Michelle approaches every situation with empathy and offers vetted, executable solutions that were formed from real life experiences rather than in textbooks. This mindful deviation is what has led to Michelle's impressive track record since the beginning of her career. She is an 11X Internationally Best-Selling Author, Certified Life/ Relationship/ Business Coach, Motivational speaker, and Multiple Minority Business Owner.

Financial growth is a key aspiration for entrepreneurs, as it signifies the success and sustainability of their ventures. However, achieving accelerated prosperity requires a strategic approach and a solid understanding of the essential steps involved. Women of color entrepreneurs especially face unique challenges on their journey towards financial prosperity. They often encounter systemic barriers that hinder access to capital, resources, and opportunities. However, with resilience, strategic planning, and a supportive ecosystem, women of color entrepreneurs can overcome these hurdles and achieve prosperity. In this discussion, we will explore key strategies and initiatives that can help women of color entrepreneurs navigate, conquer financial barriers, and unleash their financial growth potential.

Let me take a moment to introduce myself. I am Dr. Michelle S. Thomas, Founder/CEO of The Exceptional Woman Enterprise, and Co-Owner of Sixcess Industries Inc. a Parent Holding Company of multiple subsidiaries. That is who I am today, but to bring relevance to the value of information I am about to provide, we must go back in time to get a glimpse of my story.

Statistically I have checked all of the boxes that "society" deems failures. Abused, neglected, bankrupt, divorced, bad credit, single mom, laid off, and insecure. As if all of that wasn't bad, the worst of my low was the years that I BELIEVED that I was someone that was born to fail. I was raised to work hard and give everything to my career. I followed the rules to a fault but continuously found myself frustrated and unceasingly financially struggling.

As I began to concede that "this was my life", I took a position as the leader of a finance department at the company where I worked. This was not the position I was looking for but now I can say it was the position I needed to unlock my destiny. I worked directly for the Controller who was one of the most financially literate women I had ever met. She was well-respected around the industry for the excellence of her departments.

As a woman leader thriving within a male dominated industry, she recognized the importance of knowledge and the criticality of training beyond the position. Her only requirement was that anyone that she poured into must have the desire to learn, no excuses and no nonsense. I learned so much about corporate finances, profit and loss, budgets, projections, and other financial aspects. However, at the time I did not realize how much I would need that information to proficiently own the seven profitable businesses I have to date. She challenged me, stretched my expertise, and elevated my confidence within my capabilities.

That forward training is the reason for this chapter. I value this information tremendously, because someone saw something in me even when I did not see it for myself and had the foresight to pour into my career. Even as broken as I felt, although the knowledge that was being poured into me did not seem relevant to my position, I still understood that knowledge meant power.

I am writing this chapter for the next ME! The person that has a passion for their entrepreneurial journey but seems to continue hitting the same financial roadblocks. Some of the information may seem like it does not pertain directly to your business or industry, however as my previously mentioned mentor said, "Your success can only be fueled or limited by the knowledge you accept or refuse!" Through her mentoring I learned the critical lesson that financial growth is a journey that requires dedication, resilience, and continuous adaptation.

I now would like to give your business a comprehensive framework that has been utilized throughout the numerous industries and levels of my multiple businesses to build my success. Now through my network we help entrepreneurs exceed their planned successes via the same program. By implementing these steps, you can navigate the pathway into prosperity with confidence and resilience.

Build Financial Literacy and Confidence

One of the first steps for women of color entrepreneurs to overcome financial barriers is to develop strong financial literacy and confidence. This entails acquiring knowledge about financial management, understanding key financial concepts, and becoming familiar with the intricacies of business finances. Educational programs, workshops, mentorship, and networking opportunities can play a crucial role in empowering women of color entrepreneurs to navigate the financial landscape with confidence while making informed decisions.

Access to Capital and Funding Opportunities

Access to capital remains a significant challenge for women of color entrepreneurs. Traditional funding sources often lack diversity and may overlook or undervalue their ventures. To overcome this barrier, it is important to seek out alternative funding options and support networks specifically designed for women of color entrepreneurs, such as The Exceptional Woman Network! This also includes exploring grants, loans, and venture capital firms that prioritize diversity and inclusion. Additionally, building strong relationships with angel investors, crowdfunding platforms, and community development financial institutions can provide avenues for securing the necessary financial resources.

I need to take a moment to advise you of the risks of some of the aforementioned options for funding. Entrepreneurs seeking funding often turn to venture capitalists (VCs) and angel investors as potential sources of capital. While these investors can provide valuable financial support and guidance, there are also risks associated with engaging with them. Here are some of the risks that entrepreneurs may face when dealing with venture capitalists and angel investors:

1. **Loss of Control:** When entrepreneurs accept investments from VCs or angel investors, they often relinquish a portion of ownership and decision-making power in their company.
2. **Dilution of Equity:** In exchange for funding, entrepreneurs typically issue equity in their company to VCs or angel investors. Entrepreneurs need to assess the potential impact on their ownership and long-term control over their business prior to venturing into this line of funding.

3. **Pressure to Achieve Rapid Growth:** Venture capitalists often have high expectations for rapid growth and return on investment. This can create pressure on entrepreneurs to prioritize short-term growth over long-term sustainability.

4. **Misalignment of Goals and Vision:** Entrepreneurs are often passionate about their business and its long-term impact, while investors may prioritize financial returns above other considerations. This misalignment can create conflicts and make it challenging to make strategic decisions that align with the entrepreneur's vision and values.

5. **Loss of Confidentiality:** In the process of seeking funding, entrepreneurs may need to disclose sensitive information about their business. There is a risk that this information could be misused or leaked, potentially harming the competitive advantage of the company. Entrepreneurs should take precautions to protect their intellectual property and ensure they are working with reputable investors who respect confidentiality.

While these risks exist, it's important to note that not all investors pose the same level of risk. It is crucial for entrepreneurs to conduct due diligence on potential investors, assess their track record, reputation, and values, and seek legal and financial advice when negotiating investment terms. Building a strong investor-entrepreneur relationship based on trust, communication, and shared goals can mitigate some of these risks and create a supportive partnership.

Leverage Community and Networks

Creating a strong support network and leveraging community resources are vital for women of color entrepreneurs. Building connections with like-minded individuals, mentors, industry professionals, and organizations that champion diversity can offer access to valuable insights, opportunities, and potential collaborations. Joining professional associations, attending conferences, and participating in community initiatives can help establish connections and open doors to financial resources and partnerships.

Seek Mentorship and Sponsorship Programs

Mentorship and sponsorship programs tailored for women of color entrepreneurs are powerful tools in overcoming financial barriers. These programs provide guidance, support, and valuable networks that can enhance financial acumen and access to opportunities. Engaging with mentors and sponsors who have successfully navigated similar challenges can offer insights into overcoming financial hurdles and provide guidance on strategic decision-making, financial planning, and scaling ventures.

Foster Collaborative Partnerships and Alliances

Creating strategic partnerships and alliances can amplify the financial prospects for women of color entrepreneurs. By identifying organizations, businesses, and individuals with shared goals, synergies can be leveraged to access new markets, secure contracts, and explore joint ventures. Collaboration can also provide access to resources, knowledge, and expertise that may otherwise be challenging to obtain individually. By pooling resources and combining strengths, women of color entrepreneurs can overcome financial barriers and unlock new pathways to prosperity.

Overcoming financial barriers requires a multi-faceted approach that addresses the unique challenges faced by women of color entrepreneurs. By investing in financial literacy, seeking out diverse funding opportunities, leveraging networks and mentorship programs, forging collaborative partnerships, and advocating for policy change, women of color entrepreneurs can break through these barriers and achieve financial prosperity. It is crucial to foster an ecosystem that recognizes and supports the potential of women of color entrepreneurs, enabling them to thrive and contribute to economic growth and innovation. Remember, financial growth is a journey that requires dedication, resilience, and continuous adaptation. With the right mindset and implementation of these steps, entrepreneurs can unlock unprecedented levels of prosperity and success.

Chapter Twelve:

"I'm An Investor?"

RAY'CHEL WILSON, CFEI®

RAY'CHEL WILSON, FOUNDER OF RAISE THE BAR INVESTMENTS, LLC AND FOROURLASTNAMES

Ray'Chel's journey is one of turning passion into action. Through her first business venture, Raise the Bar Investments, Ray'Chel has pioneered a financial education social enterprise that empowers minorities to bridge the racial and gender wealth gap. Inspired by her own financial achievements, including leveraging cryptocurrency profits to pay off her undergraduate student loans, Ray'Chel birthed Raise the Bar Investments. Her accolades include recognition as one of 'Tulsa's Emerging 100' entrepreneurs. Armed with a degree in Public Health from The Ohio State University, a CFEI certification through the National Financial Educators Council, and a Certificate in Women's Entrepreneurship from Cornell University, Ray'Chel is a published author of the 'Black Wealth Freedom' series.

Being a first-generation individual isn't a walk in the park. Whether you've just donned that graduation cap, you're pondering your next career move, or you've stumbled upon a windfall, venturing into the world of finance can be quite a wild ride. These life experiences once made me think that investing was a realm reserved for others, far beyond my grasp. But, my perspective on investing took a U-turn when two distinctive chapters unfolded in my life.

Let's rewind to my younger years. Imagine me at 18, a college freshman, thrilled to receive my very first college refund check—an extra $800 USD in my pocket. As that sweet sum landed in my bank account, the notion of investing wasn't even a blip on my radar. Instead, I had other plans—the kind that involved a shopping spree. So, along with my roommate, we seized our checks, called an Uber, and made a beeline for the nearest mall.

Inside the well-lit confines of Foot Locker, which seemed to have a magnetic pull for financially naive students like me, I stumbled upon a trio of Timberland boots. These boots weren't just functional for Ohio's frosty winters; they were a symbol of status and style. Rather than making the prudent choice of saving or investing, I chose to splurge all that money right then and there.

Now, here's where I fess up to my financial blunder. I didn't heed the timeless advice of "pay yourself first" through savings or investments. Instead, I went all out on shopping, draining my college funds faster than you can say 'financial literacy.' It wasn't until my twenties that a light bulb went off in my head—the magic of compound interest. I realized that if I had invested just $400 of that refund check in index funds, it could have mushroomed into nearly $1,000 or more by the time I hit 35. A thousand dollars might not seem like a fortune, but having that kind of cushion can make all the difference, whether it's for a down payment on a home or pursuing your financial goals without the stress of playing catch-up.

Fast forward to the post-college phase of my life. With my degree in hand and dreams in my heart, I faced pivotal career choices. My parents had drilled into me the age-old wisdom of "secure a good job with good benefits." Amidst a sea of options— some safe, some not-so-much—I took a leap and joined Teach for America (TFA).

This path led me to Tulsa, Oklahoma, a place with historical significance as Black Wall Street. Looking back, this adventure, characterized by a paycheck that barely made ends meet, a whirlwind pace, and personal growth, taught me a vital lesson. It underscored the importance of investing in one's skills.

Through teaching, I discovered the transformative power we hold to ignite positive change within our communities. My TFA comrades and I swiftly ascended the ranks in education and related fields, making an impact and earning our keep, all thanks to the skills we honed as enthusiastic educators. More significantly, investing in skills that enrich your community is akin to planting the seeds of communal growth—a concept that resonates deeply with my upbringing, where I learned about bringing the goodness of Heaven to Earth (Matthew 6:10).

It wasn't until I paid off my student loans through investing, all while earning a salary in one of the lowest-paying states for teachers, that I could look in the mirror and declare, "I am an investor." If only I had known earlier that I could, should, and was meant to invest from the get-go. Paying off those student loans wasn't just a victory for my financial journey; it also freed up more funds for me to contribute to my community, increase my tithes and offerings at my church, and purchase services that liberated my time, enabling me to mentor and give back more generously. Investing is a tool of liberation.

These chapters of my investing saga have bequeathed me a profound lesson: Value doesn't sprout solely from saving or playing it safe. It flourishes through investing. Plunging headlong into financial assets without nurturing your skills is akin to a fitness enthusiast who skips leg day—a mistake that knows no gender.

The art of investing causes personal & financial value to thrive!

I hope my brief account of these experiences inspires you to embark on your own investment journey, commencing early and staying the course. To access valuable resources tailored for first-generation investors, please visit www.ForOurLastNames.io. Together, let's build wealth #ForOurLastNames!

Disclosures:

Information in this publication does not involve the rendering of personalized investment, insurance, tax nor legal advice but is limited to the dissemination of general educational information on financial instruments, products or services. None of the content should be viewed as an offer to buy or sell, or as a solicitation of an offer to buy or sell any of the securities discussed. A licensed, qualified, investment, insurance, tax or legal professional advisor should always be consulted before implementing any of the options presented.

LEVERAGE PILLAR

Chapter Thirteen:
"It's In Your Hands"

NIEDA WASHINGTON
Financial Coach

Nieda Washington is a licensed financial advisor and coach with over a decade and a half of experience in guiding clients towards financial recovery and prosperity. Specializing in credit restoration, money, and debt management, she has been a trusted mentor for newcomers in the finance industry since 2005.

Nieda's passion lies in empowering individuals to overcome financial setbacks and achieve their financial aspirations. Her comprehensive approach, encompassing mentorship, and personalized financial strategies, has made her an indispensable ally for those seeking to regain control of their finances and accomplish their financial objectives.

What's in your hands?

As I sit and reflect on one of the most trying times in history. I think of how resilient we are as a people. How when faced with adversities we are able to adapt and overcome. During Covid, so many lives were changed. Some were negatively impacted and some were changed for the good. I saw people build multimillion dollar businesses on social media and I saw people shift into their destinies.

I say all of this as a precursor to what I want to talk about in this chapter. I want you to take away that no matter what adversities you have faced you are stronger than you think and you're an overcomer. No matter what hand life has thrown at you. You are triumphant and can overcome anything thrown at you. How do I know this? Because, you are reading my chapter and that tells me YOU MADE IT. You are alive, so that means there is still work for you to do. So, let's get to it!

My name is Nieda Washington and they call me the Bougie Girls Money Coach. I am a Financial Advisor, Financial Consultant, Coach, speaker and your favorite money mentor for Professional women who have made financial mishaps and mistakes in the past and want to overcome adversities. I am the girl to get you from financial woes to financial abundance with…. *guess what?*

What's already in your hands.

Yes, you already hold the keys to your destiny to unlock that door of abundance and move you from a defeated to overcomer's mindset. You have the keys to go from overspending to saving and creating generational wealth. Yes, yes, yes I AM TALKING TO YOU! So, let's not delay and get right to it.

I have experienced everything from financial trauma to financial lack and abundance. I have been, as the Bible says, *abased and abound* and have learned to manage wherever I am at the time. I grew up in what we like to call the "hood" or one of the toughest neighborhoods in Philadelphia. I am not the norm to come from the "hood". I am the exception and defy all odds that have been set against people that look like me and I've been blessed to learn how money works and I am going to share some of those things with you. No worries though, if you don't get everything here just remember to follow me on social media @Nieda_washington on Instagram. You'll be sure to connect with me and get what you need.

Sometimes when we are looking to create a better life for ourselves we tend to look beyond the power that already exists in us. We tend to watch what others are doing and get caught up in the Get Rich Quick schemes that tend to be nothing but more impoverished people making others rich… when we already have the juice. The power is in your hands, and I am going to show you how to use it. How to leverage credit in order to help you create financial abundance.

Now, if your credit isn't in the best place at the moment, that's completely alright. Take this time to work on repairing your credit and if you need a little assistance feel free to reach out to me for some credit tips and my credit repair services @nieda_washington on Instagram. So, to gain a better understanding of what we are building we need to first understand: What is Generational Wealth and why do we want to create it.

Generational Wealth - also known as family wealth/ legacy wealth refers to assets passed down from one generation to the next. This wealth transfer can provide financial security and open doors of opportunity for those who inherit it. It's not just about money but, it's also about assets like real estate, stocks, businesses, and other investments.

Generational wealth can come in various forms. These assets grow over time, providing financial cushioning and enabling the next generation to build upon the foundation laid by their forbearers.

Why is Generational Wealth Important?

The significance of generational wealth cannot be understated. Here are some reasons why it's important:

1. Offers Financial Security
2. Access to Better Opportunities.
3. Wealth Accumulation.
4. Creating a Legacy.
5. Breaking the Poverty Cycle.

Now, we understand what Generational Wealth is and the importance of creating Generational Wealth. Let's discuss 5 tips on how to leverage your credit to create Generational Wealth.

Establish a Strong Credit Profile

You want to make sure you start off with a strong credit profile. Building a good credit history is important. Make sure you pay your bills on time. Make sure your utilization stays below 30% and make sure your credit is diversified.

Use Credit to Invest in Income Generating Assets

Credit can be used to purchase assets that generate income over time, such as real estate or a business. The goal is to have income from these assets exceed the cost of the debt, leading to a net gain. For instance, taking a mortgage to buy a rental property can create a steady stream of income for generations.

Leverage Business Credit

Business credit allows a business owner to borrow under the business name. By building strong business credit you can access larger amounts of capital for business growth and expansion. A thriving business can be a significant part of your generational wealth.

Consider Real Estate

Real estate is often a core component of generational wealth. You can leverage credit to invest in real estate through various credit to invest in real estate through various strategies, like property flipping or rental properties. Real estate often appreciates over time providing long term returns.

Invest in Education

Use credit to invest in your own children's education. The right education can lead to higher income opportunities, allowing for more savings and investments. For instance, taking out student loans to finance a degree in a high-demand field could lead to a high-paying job, enabling wealth accumulation.

Remember, while credit can be a powerful tool, it also carries risks. It's crucial to have a solid repayment strategy to avoid falling into a debt trap. Be sure to weigh the potential returns against the cost of borrowing before using credit to make any significant financial decisions. It's also important to note that building generational wealth involves more than just leveraging credit, saving, investing, and maintaining good financial habits.

Now that you have read how to leverage your credit. If you need help with establishing good money habits or would like a free 15-minute consultation to help get your finances in order go follow me on Instagram @nieda_washington, click the link in my bio and set up you free 15-minute consultation and while your there take advantage of my free financial workbook.

Chapter Fourteen:
"Keys To Establishing (Great) Business Credit"

D. CHERELLE COHENS, MBA
Business Funding Expert

At Business Squared LLC, we understand entrepreneurs and business owners need to develop and identify their Business Financial Future. Since 2017, we've been helping companies of all sizes respond to the need for business funding, financial structure, and resources. Our years of experience and financially tenured CEO have taught us to always make your business success our priority.

Our CEO is a 10 year Licensed Retired Banking Leader, Founder of Pitch Your Passion Pitch Competition, Founder of Heal-A-Preneur, Baltimore City Women Commissioner, SCORE Business Counselor, and a member of Delta Sigma Theta Sorority Incorporated. Due to her leadership Business Squared LLC has been funded by KIVA Baltimore, Licensed Business Credit Vendor, E-Cornell 2021 Women & Business Entrepreneurship Certified, and Better Business Bureau approved. Allow our CEO to provide you CFO Services.

I didn't know much about credit, until it was time for me to get my first place to call my own. And there it was, the email denial that I had not been accepted to a residence because my parents thought it was ok to advise me to leave my on-campus housing prematurely, due to lack of funds. I knew I had to fight, I pulled all my reports and there it was, almost 14K in debt and I HAD NO CLUE it was there. I disputed the debt and went back and forth for three months leveraging technicalities, missing information, and play on words. Before I knew it, I had cleaned my own credit up and I was proud and moved into my new place that same year. I learned that credit could keep you from your new home.

Later, working for a bank, I was asked to curate a personal credit plan to create more credit interest for clients in the community. It was no problem for me to indulge with pride and experience. I was in for a rude awakening because clients had no issues trusting me to apply, the issue was they simply lacked credit requirements. What could I do, my clients trusted me to apply but to tell them they were denied killed me. In this experience I learned the power of Secured Credit. I taught this to my clients, and showed them how they could crawl before they walked, making a deposit on their credit cards, practicing good payment habits, and graduating from secured to unsecured credit. I sold over 100 credit apps in 2015. I learned that credit literacy will change how you handle your finances and the opportunities you acquire.

Fast forward to 2017, I met Baltimore's "Mr. Business Credit", at least that's what he called himself at the time, he spent the day with me and provided the Credit Literacy about Business Credit I had NEVER heard about. He taught me all the ins and outs of non-traditional business credit and I could not believe what I was hearing!!! "I thought to myself, wait a gosh darn minute, you can build Business Credit without personal credit?!"

The answer is yes, but of course I had to do my own research. I went into deep isolation, I was knee deep into business credit education for months, learning, research case stories, other business credit educators, and how financial institutions handled non-traditional business credit.

I started my Business Credit Educator journey in 2018 and began teaching open-minded entrepreneurs that Business Credit was attainable even if you were like my clients from the bank leveraging secured credit until your personal credit reigned again. Finally, I was ready and built my own business credit profile, created vendor relationships, and leveraged credit lines to support my company's growth. However, as I was building business credit, I realized it takes money to create money opportunities, I mean not ALWAYS, but most times it does.

Business Credit is a powerful tool when approached with the proper mindset and plan of action tailored to your business goals and success. One thing for sure, it's certainly not a spectator sport, watching how other companies go after their business credit goals will not always resemble the best practices for your own company. After teaching Business Credit for over seven years and building the personal credit confidence in everyday people at the bank for over ten years, I became inspired by a three part-mindset approach to increase Business Credit Development success.

The Establish-Build-Grow Method is a mindset and implementation framework for business credit execution and ironically enough, a mindset required in life itself. The Establish-Build-Grow Method was created to inspire credit builders to take their approach to credit acceleration one step at a time over the course of a three-step process. This method was inspired by today's generation of business minds that expect instant gratification. Credit development is not an overnight process, in fact it is about strategy, action, and the vision you have for your credit. The more business owners understand that a process is required for credit development, the more success a company will have achieving their credit goals. The Establish-Build-Grow Method helps to provide a framework for the mindset and strategy necessary when beginning to execute a successful Business Credit Plan.

Let's start with step one of the Establish-Build-Grow Method for creating your Business Credit Plan, ESTABLISH. The absolute first step in your business credit development approach is all about your foundation, the basics, and the preliminary business structure you need to put in place on a ground level before even applying for credit. A great beginning thought to have when establishing your Business

Credit Plan is to complete your Business Credit Profile. Establishing your Business Credit Profile successfully is the bridge to upcoming vendor relationships that extend instant credit, help to grow your Paydex score (like a personal credit score, except for your business), and support the needs of your business. A strong Business Credit Profile is the key to borrower worthiness, trust, and a professionally presented business.

Here are some steps you can take to position your company to establish your Business Credit

Profile:

1. Analyze Personal & Business Credit Reports Assess where you are with your personal credit, then your business credit. Understanding your current credit situation is one of the first steps to establishing your business credit profile because you must first know where you are to plan strategically. Through this process you should be pulling your personal credit reports with TransUnion, Equifax, and Experian. You are entitled to one free annual credit report with all three credit bureaus every year. The reports can be found on these websites: (consumer.ftc.gov) and (annualcreditreport.com). The scores are analyzed utilizing both Vantage 3.0 & FICO.

Having a solid understanding of where your personal credit goals should always come primary to your Business Credit goals. *Addressing your Business Credit Goals by ignoring your personal credit is not encouraged.* Always have a clear understanding of your personal finances before becoming too consumed with your business finances. Your business finances are a derivative of your personal financial goals. Sometimes there can be traces of business credit in your name of which you are not aware. Be sure to pull your business credit report as well. Nav.com is a great place to start for business credit reporting. 99-650, Poor 649-600, Very Bad 599 and below.

2. Establish a legal entity with a business address. Your business must be a registered business (an LLC, Incorporation, or Partnership) to be considered for competitive business credit opportunities. A registered business shows business authority.

3. Apply for an EIN. Your entity identity number is often required for vendors, lenders, and other institutions to identify with your business especially for tax, income, and credit purposes.

4. Register Dun & Bradstreet #. This number demonstrates business credit worthiness. It is important that a business owner establishes a strong Business Credit Profile by creating a DUNS number, which stands for Data Universal Number System. While this can be done for free, it's an easy task to procrastinate and some business owners find it best to outsource technical assistance.

5. Establish positive credit history. Having a historically successful personal credit profile adds value to your Business Credit Profile because it puts you in position for access to more funding opportunities. A personal positive credit history means you can serve as a personal guarantor to your business loans/credit, which accelerates the funding process. Also, building a positive business credit history can be done non-traditionally without being dependent on personal guarantors.

6. Speak with an accountant. Accountants should be preparing you for the future financial vision of the company. This means providing tax-strategies to execute throughout the course of a year that equates to tax-benefited returns. Business credit expenses and payments are a contributory factor to these strategies.

7. Establish a Business Plan. Some lending opportunities require you to present your full business plan as a form of supporting documentation that proves the reasoning for your credit requests.

8. Develop a Website. Credit lending is all about trust and bower worthiness, establishing your company/brand at a serious level requires digital and actual presence, a website is a reference for lenders to acknowledge and confirm your company's existence and Intention.

9. Open Small Business Checking Account. The establishment of a bank account can be used as a reference to demonstrate the history of how a company does business, which can be a requirement to review for credit worthiness.

10. Purchase Business Insurance. Protecting your business with insurance limits liability on the lender's side and makes it easier to extend credit when in place.

11. Apply for a Business Credit Card. Entering your first credit application now seals that your business credit profile is complete and ready to BUILD upon.

Next, let's get into the second step to the Establish-Build-Grow Method, BUILD. What we have determined about building, is that it doesn't happen successfully without the appropriate foundation. While in step one we focused on ESTABLISH, we felt this was primary because when we BUILD in step two, it is to build upon the foundation in which we have established. BUILD, in this case simply means building a vendor, financial institution, and credit relationships. It's often recommended that credit relationships are built in a strategic manner that supports your business and credit goals.

Building successful credit accounts and relationships means:

1. Understanding application requirements prior to applying;
2. Addressing how vendor products and services serve your business needs and/or business community needs;
3. Learning how building one vendor relationship leads you to a more extensive credit relationship that supports your company more in-depth... Now that will lead you to GROWTH!

Growth is the last step in the Establish, Build, Grow Method. Growth is what happens after you establish your business credit foundation, Build is what happens when your foundation is solid, however growth is what happens when it's time to be larger and greater over time. When you are growing in your Business Credit Plan you are making decisions for the financial milestones in your company that help you scale. Your credit opportunities are focused more on strategizing on executing income generators at a high profitable level & the incorporation of Conventional Lending. Growth is what happens when you are ready to increase in volume and do business credit on a scale that closes gaps and creates more opportunity for profit and financial milestone execution within the company.

At this level, you are tackling your Business Credit Plan at a high level and you are closer to fully fulfilling your plan than the beginning stages. Normally at this phase in the plan you have established well over twelve credit relationships and majority of your execution goals have been completed, you should be close to revisiting and enhancing your current plan because you are in a state of completion.

Completing your first Business Credit Plan does not mean business credit development should subside. You simply should be reviewing your success, your losses, and your pending business goals and pressing forward with the needs that need to be met in the current day. Needs change, businesses pivot, and more goals are added, review your Business Credit Plan Annually.

The most important question through the Establish-Build-Grow Method is: *how do I leverage business credit opportunities to add value to my business?* You accept the process of the Establish-Build-Grow Method, you accept the crawls before the walks, the walks before the runs, and the runs before the sprints. This is a process during which you can easily feel discouraged when falling short in execution during the ESTABLISH and BUILD portions of the method, However, working with experts can help take you where you need to be, so you don't fall off track. You don't build personal credit overnight, same with business credit development.

Stay true to the process if you intend to build non-traditional business credit (credit not required to be personally guaranteed), go into it understanding you must establish, build, and grow.

Chapter Fifteen:

"The 3 P's to Living Your Best Life"

CECILIA BAILEY, CFED®

Ms. Bailey has more than 24 years' experience in personal finance, non-profit management, and community development. As a banker, she has been responsible for fostering community partnerships and the strategic delivery of financial education programs throughout a 15-state footprint. In addition, she is highly skilled in creating and delivering train-the-trainer programs in the financial education space.

She has a true passion for teaching and has served as a subject matter expert (SME) on the topic of personal finance and been featured on CBS42 in Birmingham as a personal finance expert. This passion led her to obtain her Certified Financial Educator® (CFEd ®) designation, that is recognized by FINRA.

Her work in personal finance has led to educating, training and coaching thousands of families and individuals across the country to include youth, young adults, adults and people in transition. She published her first book in November 2018 entitled, Money Boot Camp: A Guide to Whipping Your Finances into Shape.

Who really cares about personal finance and what good is it serving when another black man's life was literally choked out of him? It was a modern day lynching the way George Floyd died. On May 25, 2020 the murderer used a knee instead of a rope. Yes, I was incensed like so many other people. You can't just say Americans because the whole world saw and responded.

As a personal finance expert, trainer, coach and author I began to question whether or not people cared about a budget or credit score in lieu of what was taking place in this country. I began to question whether or not I had done enough or how I would fight the injustices and hatred in this world with conversations about money. But what I had to be reminded of is that if economic opportunity was the great equalizer, then I was creating a bridge to get there by teaching personal finance. I was instrumental in laying the foundation of financial success and removing the veil of confusion such as questions like, "Where do I start?" and "How do I get there?"

So what have you laid aside in your frustration or anger? Like me, you've probably called into question your dreams or goals when you witness injustice in this country. But at the end of the day, no matter what we do it will take money to live and thrive. For that reason, I reignited the fire of my purpose and began to teach more because helping people to secure a financial future has value in this world.

Although it cannot bring a loved one back, money can assist in the grieving process when we bury someone on Friday and don't have to go to work on Tuesday because we have proper life insurance. It gives us room to fight when we know our bills are paid and we have more money than month. When I lost my husband in 2007, after three short years of marriage, our insurance policy carried me for five years after his death. FIVE years!

In a January 2023 study, Forbes Advisor found that "In the event of losing a primary wage earner, nearly half (44%) of American households would encounter significant financial difficulties within six months. More than a quarter (28%) would reach this point in only one month." How secure is your financial future?

My mission is very simple – to inspire hope and action for you to live your best life by adhering to these basic money principles.

1) Plan your future
2) Pay who you owe
3) Protect your legacy

Plan your future by understanding your money scripts and setting goals that inspire you. Money Scripts is a term coined and introduced by Brad Klontz, a thought leader in the world of financial therapy.

Simply stated, these are the unconscious beliefs about money rooted in our childhood that ultimately shapes our financial health. I grew up in a household where we didn't talk about money with intentionality but when it did come up money seemed to be scarce or carefully allocated. As a result, my money script aligns with money vigilance because I want to talk about money with great intention.

The main types are Money Avoidance, Money Worship, Money Status and Money Vigilance. Although they sound pretty self-explanatory, I'll provide some context.

Money avoidance might stem from perceiving money to be evil or a taboo topic. You might have grown up not talking about money in your house and as a result avoid any planning around financial stability or security.

Money worship can present it itself as the total opposite, instead of avoiding it, it would become the solution for everything. Your happiness, your fulfillment and the end to all of your problems. I don't necessarily see it as "worshiping" money as much as it being the primary solution to everything.

Money status takes worship to another level because it primarily says that money defines your self-worth. You associate higher incomes, the latest fashion and expensive trends with a higher value over what may really bring you true joy and pleasure.

Money vigilance seems to be what we should be aiming for because it tends to describe someone that is responsible and intentional about their finances, but to the point where it can be perceived as obsessive. A money vigilant person is highly focused on making sure they're hitting their goals but this oftentimes comes at the expense of enjoying their hard work and diligence.

When you understand how you perceive money you will more likely set goals in alignment with those beliefs. There is no right or wrong, you just have to know. Your goals will help keep you focused, determine your needs versus wants and help you achieve financial success. Write them down. Properly categorize them from short-term, medium-term and long-term goals. Make them SMART --specific, measurable, attainable, realistic/relevant and time-bound.

For example, I set a goal to not use credit cards at all for 90 days starting on March 1 st in order to understand more about my psychology of having credit card debt and living within my means. Yes, the personal finance expert still be having challenges in these money streets! Of course on March 3rd I had a $1200 car repair that I would have normally put on a credit card, but instead I paid cash. It was difficult but part of my journey.

Pay who you owe, including yourself. Three things I want you to do here, create a budget, save with intention and monitor your credit. A spending plan (or budget) allows you to create a strategy of how you spend and save your money. Period. People tend to shy away from the term budget because it sounds restrictive.

We all need some guardrails to keep us focused on the goals we're trying to achieve. It's quite simple in theory –calculate your income, track your spending, list your expenses and pay your bills on time. In reality you might have to delete your favorite shopping apps, unsubscribe from some retailers and limit your brunching to twice a month instead of every Saturday and Sunday.

Or you may have to increase your income because brunching with your crew adds value and is a priority in your life.

Paying yourself first is a term we use to prioritize saving. A study by the Federal Reserve Bank indicated that it would be a challenge for almost 40% of Americans to come up with $400 in case of an emergency, without having to borrow or sell something. You may find this hard pressed yourself, but we still live in a gig economy where we can make extra money by installing an app on our phone --- taking surveys, conducting studies, selling online, creating a course. It can be done!

You want to also know your numbers ---your credit scores, your debt-to-income ratios, your fixed expenses, your variable expenses, your net worth and for some, your total income. You never want to find yourself at the mercy of a lender because you haven't done your homework.

Apps like Credit Karma can help you monitor your credit. But also, credit card providers and many banks offer a look at your credit score for free. At annualcreditreport.com you can download a free copy of your credit report every year. Keep in mind that this does not include the credit score, but a complete copy of the report itself.

Lastly, protect your legacy by ensuring that you have adequate life insurance, a will and an estate plan. Many people feel as though they don't have much to leave behind, provided they even want to do that. Having a written plan ensures the stated disposition of your assets. When my dad passed in 2020, he had nothing in place. As a matter of fact, he had insured inoperable cars and boats, but not his own life. I'm not certain what my dad really wanted. Would he prefer that my siblings had kept the house rather than sell it? Did he have a charity he favored to donate his tools and other household items?

That we will never know because he left very little instructions. He did, in the eleventh hour, agree to draft a simple will to take care of the major assets. But imagine if that conversation had taken place three years ago instead of three weeks before he'd taken his last breath. More thought could have been given to how he wanted to see his legacy play out. You have the opportunity to do that. My request is simple:

1) Understand your money mindset and set some realistic goals.
2) Create a spending plan, monitor your credit and know your numbers.
3) Get life insurance/review your existing plan and then help someone else get a policy.

Sometimes we need an accountability partner or coach to help guide us on our financial

journey. Let's have a conversation.

Cecilia R. Bailey, CFEd®

Author, Money Boot Camp: A Guide to Whipping Your Finances into Shape

ceciliarbailey@gmail.com or IG @ceciliarbailey

Chapter Sixteen:
"Leveraging Debt to Achieve Wealth"

ZINNIA ADAMS, MBA, CFEI®
Financial Empowerment Educator and Speaker

PERSPECTIVES

Zinnia Adams is a trailblazing fin-fluencer and the Executive founder of Perspectives, a personal finance education brand created to help high-achieving women overcome money mistakes and breakthrough bad spending habits to achieve financial stability. Perspectives consist of providing realistic solutions to real-life money problems by fostering an environment that makes personal finance concepts relatable and helps students gain confidence in their finances without losing themselves.

Zinnia leveraged her own experiences, knowledge, and education to become a Personal Finance Coach, Consultant, and Motivational Speaker. Whether she is performing as a conference Keynote speaker, conducting online courses, offering financial coaching, or providing consulting services, she meets individuals at their level and reduces the complexity and secrecy around money conversations. Her transformative work continues to make waves in the realm of personal finance education.

If you were to take a poll of the top 100 wealthiest people on the planet, you'd discover that each one of them, without exception, used real estate as a stepping stone on their path to riches.

Born into a world where financial wisdom wasn't handed down, my fumbles with money were less about recklessness and more the product of an education I hadn't received. My life took a sharp turn when I became a mom at seventeen. Six days later, I was graduating high school, the baby belly I carried at prom now a baby in my arms. I was stubborn, checking out of the hospital even when they told me I shouldn't, just to make sure I wouldn't flunk out of high school and spend my summer stuck in a classroom. Life was different now, I needed daycare in order to attend summer classes.

Scared? Sure. But mostly, I was clueless about what to do next, especially when it came to money. My own mom had me when she was seventeen, and I was her third child. For us, life was about getting by, not getting ahead. The world of personal finance was a mystery to me. Little did I know life was about to take me on a ride.

With more questions in my head than I had answers for and more weight on my shoulders than any teenager should bear, I entered adulthood. Ready or not, my journey had begun.

At eighteen, I secured my first apartment. My knowledge about money and credit was pretty much zero, but that didn't stop me. I was practically bursting with excitement; I furnished the entire apartment from Rent-A-Center and hand-me-downs just in time for my daughter's first birthday party. Showing off my furnished home to the party guests, I felt on top of the world. But then the world turned upside down. I lost my job, and everything went haywire. Without a paycheck, the rent became an impossible task. Job hunting was a challenge, especially without a place for my daughter to go.

I maxed out my credit cards, trying to keep us going, buying odds and ends and ignoring the stack of bills on my table. I didn't grasp how bad things were, and I was spending way more than I should have. Eventually, it all fell apart. Before I knew it, we were getting evicted because I couldn't cover the rent.

There I was at nineteen: no money, no job, no home, and a one-year-old daughter depending on me. I was still determining where our belongings would end up, and where we would go. Luckily, a friend of mine took us in, giving us her pull-out couch to sleep on and a chance for me to find my feet again. But during that time, I was wrestling with myself. I was mad at myself for letting this happen, for getting us into this mess. And as if things weren't bad enough, the credit card companies started hounding me for the money I owed them. I knew deep down that this wasn't how life was supposed to be.

Enough was enough. I was determined to give my daughter a better life, free from the struggles I'd endured. I was clueless about how to do it but was dead set on figuring it out. I promised myself we'd never be left homeless again. Something within me shifted, and a spark was ignited. It was as though my ambition had come alive, a flame that refused to be extinguished.

I knew I was meant for more, so I sprang into action.

First, I needed a stable income to put a roof over our heads. We lived with my friend for about a year, and I spent that time self-correcting my credit and planning for the next apartment we'd call home. The journey to financial stability had begun. Slowly but surely, I was building a life, a sturdy foundation for me and my daughter.

After we were stable again and in our own place, I turned my attention to learning about money and how to use it to craft a better future. I'd seen others in the media who'd figured it out. I thought, 'There has to be a way.' So, I dove into books, absorbing knowledge like a sponge and applying what I'd learned. The more I learned, the more my mindset shifted. My confidence bloomed, and my determination to achieve grew stronger. My dreams got bigger, and so did my actions.

It was still a tough battle. Growing up poor in the city, wealth seemed foreign, as if it belonged to another world. I'd always felt out of place in rooms filled with successful people. This made me aim for just enough to pay the bills, feeling undeserving of wealth. Struggles and homelessness - that was the life I knew. But things were about to change.

My mind expanded as I learned about money and how it should be used. It felt as though someone was pouring in a waterfall of new ideas. I was enlightened and empowered. I realized money was a tool meant to be leveraged to reach financial goals. This hunger to learn more ways to use money became my new obsession.

The journey I undertook wasn't just about surviving. It was about transforming. I transformed from a teenager who was evicted, jobless, and maxed out on credit to someone who managed to single handedly put herself through college, graduating in 2014 with a Bachelor's degree in Business without a single penny of debt hanging over her head. Later on, to achieve her M.B.A. in Finance, and not only did I pay off some debt. - I annihilated a staggering $50,000 of it.

I wasn't content with merely surviving. I aimed to thrive. I took control of my financial destiny, learning to wield debt not as a burden but as a powerful tool for creating wealth and paving the way to success. Real estate investment was my new playground, and debt was my silent partner.

I don't keep these battle-tested strategies to myself. I have become a Certified Financial Education Instructor, guiding others through their own financial mazes, helping them vanquish their money mistakes, wipe out their debts, and build wealth.

My name has graced the pages of major publications like Fidelity, Go Banking Rates, and NTD Good Morning. I've gone from evicted to invited, traveling the globe to share the vital message of personal finance education.

My change didn't just help me. It became, and still is, a shining light guiding others. I don't want anyone to feel alone on this journey without the right tools to help them.

One of the proudest moments of my financial journey was buying my first investment property. Even though it was only $40k, I financed it. That's right, after paying off $50k in debt, I got myself $30k in debt again. But trust me; it made sense. Just keep reading.

Not all debt is the same. Some is good, some is bad. Good debt helps you build wealth or improve your finances. Bad debt? That's the kind that you can't afford or doesn't give you any long-term benefits; it just takes away from your paycheck.

The price of real estate is rising. And the smartest way to buy real estate and succeed is to use debt. It lets you buy bigger properties and grow your wealth quicker. Can you picture trying to save up $400,000 from your paycheck? It would take forever! But with financing, you have so many more choices. Instead of using $40k in cash on my first property, I used that money for down payments on two places – a single-family home and a multi-unit building.

There are many ways to use debt to make money in real estate. Buying the property, fixing it up, repairs and replacements, and financing big purchases for the property are just a few examples.

The first thing I did was to get a handle on my numbers. How much was I making and spending each month? I made a debt repayment plan to pay off my debt and figured out how much I could set aside from each paycheck for real estate. I worked like crazy to boost my credit score so I could get financing. All the while, I studied real estate investing to learn different strategies and figure out which one would work best for me and my goals. And it's okay if you need help with all this.

The most important thing is to take action. Don't get stuck just thinking about everything. You have to jump in, make a move, and start changing things.

Every time you buy a new property, ensure the rent covers all the debt and monthly costs. This includes things like landscaping, managing the property, taxes, utilities, and the mortgage. With this strategy, the mortgage gets paid off without using your money. Leave your salary to invest, start a business, or find other ways to boost your finances. With the right planning and math, you can use this strategy to build wealth over and over.

All it takes is the proper game plan to change how you view and use debt.

The transformation from being frightened of debt to seeing it as an asset can be a game-changer. By learning more about finances, changing the way you think, and embracing the idea of abundance, you, too, can make this shift. Remember, it's all about viewing debt as a tool that can be effectively used to create wealth.

My story serves not only as a testimony but proof. My journey was imperfect and had more twists and turns than a roller coaster. However, I changed my money story. Take that as a lesson. No matter where you are, you can rewrite your money story one goal at a time. Now it's up to you to take these lessons and apply them in your own life. With the right mindset and strategies, the road to financial stability and success are within reach.

Chapter Seventeen:
"The Credit Catalyst: Transforming Debt into Wealth"

DR. TIFFANEY WILLIAMS
Wealth Strategist

Dr. Tiffaney Williams stands as an unstoppable force of nature, renowned for her tireless efforts both locally and internationally. She has garnered widespread acclaim, receiving the esteemed honor of a lifetime achievement award twice, recognized by distinguished leaders including those from the Biden and Obama administrations. Notably, she was recently granted the 44th Presidential Legacy Lifetime Achievement Award during Black History Month, celebrating her exceptional contributions. Her extraordinary accomplishments were further highlighted when she was chosen as one of the recipients of the 40 under 40 Elite USA Global award in New York City. Serving as a member of the Forbes Council for coaches and finance, ForbesBLK council, NSBA trustee, and Council member, Dr. Tiffaney Williams continues to make her mark.

Notably, she earned the title of Global Entrepreneur of the Year, awarded by the International Institute of Influencers in Dubai. Beyond the accolades, her story is one of resilience and determination. Dr. Tiffaney Williams channels her experiences to inspire individuals in correctional and juvenile facilities worldwide, spanning from prisons in Los Angeles to those in South Africa. Her message resonates with hope and empowerment, a testament to her unwavering dedication to creating positive change.

An innovative thought leader, Dr. Tiffaney Williams provides diverse business strategies to emerging leaders and seasoned professionals alike. Her expertise centers on educating individuals about becoming their own financial foundation and mastering the concept of "Owning Nothing and Controlling Everything" through Trust living, sovereignty, and effective business incorporation with expedited business credit options. Her mission is to repair, restore, rebuild, and educate. Her passion permeates every project she embraces.

I am a person who prides herself on being real and straightforward personally and professionally. I believe in the power of resilience, redemption and perseverance. These are qualities that one needs in their personal life, professional life and yes even as it relates to their financial journey. If it's one thing I know, "life happens" to everyone. So before I jump into this juicy content, allow me to share a bit of my backstory so that you will know why I have so passionately pursued leveraging and mastering credit to build wealth!

You might be wondering what led me to dive into this industry and whether achieving seven-figure success was easy for me. Let me introduce you to the person I was before becoming Dr. Tiffaney. I'm a Detroit native, raised by a single mother in a struggling community. My father battled drug addiction since I was just two years old. My early life was marred by not only poverty but also mental and physical abuse from my mother, even to the extent of having guns pointed at my head and being subjected to hurtful words that no child should endure. At 16, I experienced the trauma of rape, an event that left a lasting scar on my soul.

In my early twenties, I hit rock bottom, overwhelmed by one trauma after another. I found myself in a dark place where I attempted to end my own life. But it seemed that a higher power had different plans for me. I would often ask, "Why won't you let me die?" The answer, I came to understand, was that there was purpose within my pain.

Desperate to feel like I belonged, I turned to the streets and became involved in selling drugs for over a decade, leading to a series of legal troubles. Astonishingly, even while living as a felony fugitive for five years, I achieved remarkable milestones. I published my first book, which became a #1 bestseller on Amazon. I founded a non-profit organization dedicated to helping troubled teen girls who were like myself. I spoke on stages and shared my story in juvenile facilities and women's prisons all while living in the shadows to not be caught.

After gaining recognition for my contributions to the community, I established strong relationships with several political officials who not only helped me manage my affairs but also worked diligently to have my legal record expunged and cleared. I can't help but see this as nothing short of divine purpose.

I often tell others that success is not about where you start; it's about where you choose to continue and finish. Wealth building had always been a dream of mine, driven by the scarcity I experienced in my early life. Despite being labeled an underdog, destined to fail, end up incarcerated, or worse, I held onto the belief instilled in me by my beloved grandmother. She always told me that I was destined for greatness, and I clung to that belief.

My life's mission became clear – to be everything I needed for myself, my son, and those whose paths crossed mine by divine assignment. Success, to me, isn't merely about money; it's about living free from fear, doubt, and disbelief. True wealth, I've come to realize, is the ability to explore the world and experience all it has to offer– and leveraging can be instrumental in doing so!

In today's dynamic financial landscape, credit has become a powerful tool for individuals and businesses alike to create wealth and achieve their financial goals. In this chapter, we will explore the strategies and techniques to leverage credit effectively, focusing on both personal and business credit. We will delve into the success rates of businesses for men and women, the concept of using Other People's Money (OPM) to accumulate wealth, and the keys to making yourself bankable. Additionally, we will uncover the methods to build business credit, how to personally guarantee and leverage credit for asset accumulation, high-level opportunities for individuals and business owners, the importance of diversification in assets, and ultimately, the pathways to creating generational wealth and passive income. Let's embark on this journey of financial empowerment.

Section 1: The Power of Credit and Statistics

Credit can be a catalyst for wealth creation, but it is crucial to understand the numbers and trends that support this notion. Studies have shown that businesses owned by women tend to be highly successful, with a recent report revealing that women-led companies achieve a 35% higher return on investment compared to their male counterparts. This success can be attributed to various factors such as adaptability, strong communication skills, and a focus on long-term sustainability. By recognizing these statistics, women can leverage their credit and business acumen to tap into funding opportunities and drive their businesses forward.

Section 2: Monetizing OPM for Wealth Accumulation

The concept of leveraging Other People's Money (OPM) is a time-tested strategy for wealth creation. By utilizing OPM, individuals and businesses can magnify their financial capabilities and seize profitable opportunities that would otherwise be out of reach. One effective way to achieve this is through strategic partnerships, banks or credit unions (you must qualify.) Building banking relationships is a sure way to maximize the opportunity for high credit worthiness. What does that look like? Keeping large amounts constantly flowing through your account, no overdrafts, bounced checks, insufficient funds, or charge backs. Create an A+ score with each institution. Second best is where you collaborate with investors or lenders who provide the necessary capital in exchange for a share of the profits. Another avenue is venture capital, where investors inject funds into promising startups in exchange for equity. By adopting these approaches, you can harness the power of OPM to accelerate your wealth accumulation.

Section 3: Becoming Bankable: Fundability Factors

To successfully leverage credit, it is essential to make yourself "bankable" – an attractive prospect for lenders and investors. Several factors contribute to your fundability, including a strong credit history, a solid business plan, collateral assets, financial statements, business profitable tax returns and bank statements that compliment your paper trail of success. It displays your ability to generate consistent cash flow. By meticulously managing your personal and business finances, maintaining a favorable credit score, and building a compelling case for your venture's profitability, you enhance your chances of securing credit at favorable terms.

Section 4: Building Business Credit and Leveraging Personal Guarantees

Establishing and nurturing your business credit is vital for leveraging credit effectively. Begin by registering your business as a separate legal entity, obtaining an Employer Identification Number (EIN), and opening (several) business accounts. Consistently paying bills and debts on time, diversifying credit sources, and maintaining a low credit utilization under 30% these are fundamental principles to build strong business credit. Moreover, you can leverage your personal credit and guarantee to secure initial financing for your business. As your business credit strengthens, you can gradually reduce personal guarantees and rely solely on the creditworthiness of your corporation or enterprise. Join my mailing list at www.whoistiffaneywilliams.com to obtain 5 complimentary companies for funding, credit, loans, or lines of credit catered to new and existing business owners.

Section 5: High-Level Opportunities for Individuals and Business Owners

In today's interconnected world, high-level opportunities abound for individuals and business owners to expand their wealth. These opportunities include investing hard assets! What most individuals don't INNERSTAND is all assets made by God are the highest level of wealth building. That's land, oil, commodities such as Gold and silver, then real estate, stocks, learning trades such as trading forex, venturing into the realm of entrepreneurship through franchising or acquisitions; exploring angel investing or venture capital; and engaging in strategic partnerships or joint ventures. By staying informed about market trends, networking, and seeking guidance from financial experts, you can identify and capitalize on these high-level opportunities to propel your financial growth.

a. **Entrepreneurship:** Embarking on an entrepreneurial journey can provide significant opportunities for wealth creation. By identifying gaps in the market, developing innovative products or services, and scaling operations, individuals can build successful businesses and generate substantial wealth.

b. **Technology and Innovation:** Embracing technological advancements and harnessing innovation can lead to transformative opportunities. Individuals and business owners can leverage emerging technologies, such as artificial intelligence, blockchain, or renewable energy, to create groundbreaking ventures and capture significant market share.

Section 6: The Importance of Asset Diversification

Asset diversification is a vital strategy to mitigate risks and optimize wealth creation. Key considerations include:

a. **Balancing Risk and Reward:** Diversify your assets across different classes, such as stocks, bonds, real estate, and commodities. This helps distribute risk and ensures that potential losses in one area can be offset by gains in others.

b. **Geographic and Sectoral Diversification:** Expand your investment portfolio to include assets from different geographic regions and sectors. This minimizes exposure to specific economic conditions and industry fluctuations, enhancing long-term stability.

Section 7: Building Assets and Creating Generational Wealth

Building assets and creating generational wealth require a comprehensive approach and long-term vision. Strategies include:

a. **Strategic Saving and Investing:** Develop disciplined saving habits and allocate funds towards investments that generate passive income and appreciate over time. Utilize compounding returns to accelerate wealth accumulation.

b. **Business Ownership and Succession Planning:** Establish and grow a successful business that can be passed down to future generations. Implement robust succession plans to ensure the continuity of wealth and business operations.

Conclusion

By implementing these business credit hacks, entrepreneurs and business owners can expedite the growth of their business credit profiles. Building strong business credit opens doors to favorable financing terms, supplier relationships, and other financial opportunities, enabling business growth and success. Remember to approach business credit management with professionalism, discipline, and a focus on long-term financial stability.

If I could leave you with anything, it would be this: "Always strive to be and do your absolute best." The negative voices and doubters shouldn't hold any weight in your journey. I've personally gone from being that little girl, *Tiffaney Williams*, who felt like a reject, to becoming Dr. Tiffaney Williams, a person with global partnerships even in places where English isn't spoken. I'm involved in shaping wealth on a global scale, and I've played a role in driving economic transformations in various countries. I know that at times, the path ahead may seem long and daunting, like you'll never reach your destination. But trust me when I say that if you keep walking, you'll eventually find yourself exactly where you need to be.

Guys, if you would like to connect with me to see what services or course we provide at the Wealth Concierge, here is my social media Facebook: Tiffaney Williams, Instagram: @Drtiffaneywilliams LinkedIn: Tiffaney Williams, or my website: www.whoistiffaneywilliams.com

Always remember "Procrastination is the key to being Unsuccessful".

PROTECT PILLAR

Chapter Eighteen:

"Breaking Down the Tax Burden: How to Stay Ahead of the IRS"

SHAN-NEL D. SIMMONS, MBA, EA
Founder and Tax Specialist

Shan-Nel D. Simmons, EA MBA, is a seasoned accounting and finance professional with over 20 years of experience which includes being a former IRS agent. She has saved clients hundreds of thousands of dollars through her expertise in tax and financial consulting.

As the Founder and CEO of Nel Tax and Financial Solutions, Shan-Nel represents clients before the IRS. She is also a published author, sharing her knowledge in books including one about the speaking industry and one on her personal journey from employee to entrepreneur. Shan-Nel's accomplishments have been recognized by notable publications and organizations. Outside of work, she prioritizes her roles as a wife, mother, and community service member.

If you ever need a sign to confirm if your personal or business finances are profitable, owing taxes year after year is a clear indicator that you mastered the skill of making more money. But the burden of owing taxes is also a recurring reminder that you must make decisions about your overall finances that will require you to make tough choices, to stand by your own wealth intentions, and to change your habits if you are to ever get ahead and stay ahead of your tax burdens. So, let's discuss some of the reasons why your tax debt continues to be an issue and explore practical ways you can end the cycle of your tax burdens to start mastering this part of your money.

Reason No. 1 – Failure to Pay Estimated Taxes

For those of you who worked as an employee, or still work as an employee, you are comfortable with the concept of your taxes being paid per pay period as withholdings. So, when you file your tax return, you are used to either owing less taxes than what you should have to pay, owing nothing, or even receiving a refund because payroll made those tax payments for you from your pay each pay period throughout the year.

However, for those of you who receive other sources of income that are not subject to withholdings, such as self-employment income, interest income, or rental income, to name a few, you may be required to make the payments for the taxes yourself during the year. If you are required to pay the taxes yourself, these payments are known as the estimated tax payments (or commonly known as quarterly taxes or "quarterlies").

Failure to pay your estimated taxes throughout the year will result in owing all the taxes when it is time for you to file your tax return as well as subject you to additional penalties and interest. In other words, you might pay even more of your money to the IRS, and no one wants to do that.

Your solution: Make your estimated tax payments timely and throughout the year. Making those payments prevent penalties and interest, lessen (or eliminate) your tax debt, and provides you with a sense of certainty that you are on top of your taxes.

The IRS has a free tool you can use to compute how much your federal estimated taxes are each quarter at www.irs.gov/individuals/tax-withholding-estimator. It is not recommended to use the tool if you have a pension but no job, are a nonresident alien citizenship status, or if your taxes are complex, such as if you have long-term capital gains, qualified dividends, or other items not handled by the tool. In these instances, it might be best to consult with a qualified tax professional.

Your state might also require you to make state estimated tax payments, and you will need to check with the taxing authority of each state you might owe taxes to determine how much you owe and how to submit those payments. Each state may have different due dates as well. For federal estimated tax payments, you can submit the payment at www.irs.gov/payments/direct-pay.

Reason No. 2 – Overlooking Tax Deductions and Credits

Tax deductions and credits typically require some kind of proof that you qualify to claim it. It could be a receipt, an invoice, a form, an approval letter; but something is usually required for you to provide your tax professional to claim the deduction and the credit – and some of you will believe that "little piece" will not make a difference.

Forgetting those additional documents (or not mentioning additional details about your financial transaction) is like literally leaving money on the table. For example, receipts for those education expenses in addition to the form 1098-T showing the tuition paid for college could be the difference of getting the maximum credit instead of a partial credit.

Another example is maintaining the contractor statements and invoices for every time an improvement is made to your residence. This may shield additional gains from being taxable income and allow you to possibly have even more tax-free money.

Lastly, for the entrepreneurs, an example would be not claiming the depreciation expense for furniture or equipment you convert from personal to business use because it was originally purchased as your personal item. It may not seem significant to you, but that single document (or the mere mentioning of what happened with your financial situation to your tax professional) could be the difference of you owing taxes to owing less or not owing at all. Your solution: Consider everything to have a possible tax benefit. Allow research to rule out if something is ineligible for a deduction or a credit.

This is not encouraging you to deduct everything or to claim every credit. But you should always consider ways to maximize deduction and credit opportunities and confirm if you qualify to use them to your benefit. Doing so can reduce your tax debt and sometimes result in a refund instead.

Make sure to keep your documents in a secure place and have them available when it is time to prepare your tax return. If applicable, be ready to share with a tax professional additional information around your transactions as sometimes what you do not think is important could result in lowering your taxes.

Reason No. 3 – Changes in the Tax Law

Let's say you are withholding taxes, maximizing deductions and credits that you are eligible to claim, and you are even paying estimated tax payments – and somehow you still owe taxes!

Every year the tax law changes. Those changes can cause reduction or complete removal of tax credits and deductions. If those credits or deductions are reduced or removed, it may result in you owing more taxes on your income. The same applies when the tax rates increase.

When the tax rates increase, you will usually first feel its impact by having lower take-home pay from your wages for those who receive paychecks. Otherwise, if the tax rate increases due to tax law changes, you may owe more taxes on your taxable income.

Your solution: Having a Living Tax Plan that you revisit throughout the year. During the year, Congress will alter the tax laws to address changes in the country's economy and to handle the government's budget goals. Knowing this, even with the best of plans, if Congress (or other tax authorities) make changes to tax laws that apply to your financial circumstances, for the immediate change you will need to update your tax plan to work with the new laws.

The next possible solution would be to contact your elected officials and inform them of the financial burden (or administrative burden or both) created by the tax law changes allowed to pass into law. You can find your elected officials by using your address at www.house. gov/representatives/find-your-representative.

The long-term solution will be to vote and support political officials with your best interest in mind. Always remember that our elected officials work for US, and their jobs are to serve the people they represent for all matters – including your taxes.

These are just three of many reasons why your taxes may burden you year after year. You can break the cycle of what really is happening – being unprepared and scared. Owing taxes means you are a person who has taxable income. Whatever is too complex for you, there are qualified tax professionals to handle it for you. What must shift now are your methods of managing your taxable income must change to doing what is right while taking full advantage of all legal opportunities to minimize your tax burden, and you are fully capable of doing that.

Disclosures:
Information in this publication does not involve the rendering of personalized investment, insurance, tax nor legal advice but is limited to the dissemination of general educational information on financial instruments, products or services. None of the content should be viewed as an offer to buy or sell, or as a solicitation of an offer to buy or sell any of the securities discussed. A licensed, qualified, investment, insurance, tax or legal professional advisor should always be consulted before implementing any of the options presented.

Chapter Nineteen:
"The 9 to 5 Hustle"

MIA BARTEE, MBA, RFC®
Registered Financial Consultant | Total Rewards Leader | Human Capital
Management | Employee Benefits Ambassador | Financial Wellness Strategist and
Advocate

My Passion: I developed a passion for financial literacy when I began working in banking and finance during my undergraduate program. Later in my career I began managing 401K plans, which piqued my interest in developing strategies to educate employees about their Defined Contribution plans, and teaching them how to manage their assets, liabilities, cash-flow and insurances with a goal of reducing stress and increasing financial freedom and opportunity.

My Purpose: I use my passion by working with organizations to create equitable, robust, and accessible employee benefit packages at an affordable cost. When corporations adopt a collaborative approach to total rewards programs, it is a win-win for both parties. The organization becomes more competitive as they attract and retain talent, employees become better consumers of their healthcare, and more importantly, associates become financially competent.

The New Deal

If you are a millennial born between 1981 and 1996, chances are you were told to go to college so you could get a good job. And a good job wasn't just any job. A good job was one in the public sector (i.e., city, state, federal government) because it provided a decent wage with a pension.

Unfortunately, before the ink could dry on your diploma, you realized the dream you were sold was outdated. The world our parents were familiar with had completely evolved. The cost of living had significantly risen. Further, the extensive application process, antiquated technology, and lower wages made public sector jobs a very unattractive pursuit. You graduated into the Information Age, which meant that technology impacted all facets of your life – including business practices.

The year was 2004, and I had just graduated from Towson University with a bachelor's degree in communications and a minor in business. What I hoped would be an exciting time, was instead a season of overwhelming depression, self-doubt, and fear. In today's terms, I was experiencing post-grad depression. I constantly pondered the questions "passion or survival?", "how am I going to make it in this world?", "will I be successful?", "will I become a homeowner?", and so much more.

Like many young adults at the time, I decided to pursue a career in Corporate America. I appreciated the job security, competitive salary, attractive benefit package, and career development opportunities. I figured if I was going to work for someone, I needed it to be mutually beneficial.

My first post-grad job was at an investment firm. There I learned the importance of paying yourself first and leveraging your workplace benefits. This was the new corporate hustle and there was never a better time to become financially competent.

Have Your Own Back

According to the National Institute on Retirement Security, only 54% of Black and Asian employees aged 25-63 work for a retirement sponsoring employer, compared to 62%of white employees. While disappointing, this statistic is not surprising as it highlights existing social and economic disparities amplified in the private sector.

After the Revenue Act of 1978, the private sector did away with Defined Benefit plans (i.e., Pensions), Defined Contribution plans (i.e., 401K's) became the new standard retirement savings plan for American workers. This essentially transferred the risk from the employer to the employee, leaving them to bear all the responsibility of managing their investments and saving for retirement. Although 401K plans have great tax advantages and the ability to gain high returns, it requires a certain level of investment knowledge, and unfortunately, if you don't come from money or understand how money works, you're likely not aware of how to invest.

The new world made it more apparent that you must have your own back!

Pay Yourself First

Regardless of your education level or socioeconomic status, if you reside in the United States, your goal should be to increase your earnings and lower your taxable income. Too often, we get caught up in just paying our bills; however, there are major benefits to paying yourself first. By leveraging your workforce savings plan, you're able to decrease your taxable income, keep more of your money in your pocket, and save for your future-it's a win-win!

Leverage Your Workplace Savings

The most common type of workplace retirement savings plan is a Defined Contribution Plan (i.e.,401K). A 401K is a company-sponsored retirement plan. Employees can contribute to their 401K through pre-taxed payroll contributions, and the employer will typically match a portion of your contribution. In addition, some employers offer Roth 401K's, which allow employees to contribute after tax money and the account grows on a tax-free basis.

To understand the 401K-match concept, here's an example:

An employer may have a match formula that provides a match of 100% of the 1st 6% the employee contributes to their 401K. This means if an employee has an annual salary of $50,000 and contributes 6% of their salary (i.e., $3,000), the employer will provide a matching contribution of $3,000, giving the employee an aggregate annual total of $6,000 in their 401K. This allows you to maximize your savings!

In addition, there are great tax advantages of contributing to your workplace savings account. See the below illustration that shows two employees who have the same annual salary; however, one contributes to their 401K and the other doesn't. You'll notice the individual who contributes to their retirement account decreases their taxable income and has a higher take home pay. It literally pays to pay yourself first!

VALUE OF PRE-TAX BENEFITS

Example: Employee earning $30,000 annually, paying $200/month for benefits

	Without Pre-Tax Benefits	With Pre-Tax Benefits
Gross Pay	$30,000	$30,000
Insurance Deductions/401(k) Contributions	$0	$2,400
Taxable Income	**$30,000**	**$27,600**
Taxes at 25%	$7,500	$6,900
After-Tax Income	**$22,500**	**$20,700**
After-Tax Payment for Benefits	$2,400	$0
Take-home Pay	**$20,100**	**$20,700**
INCREASE IN TAKE-HOME PAY		**+$600**

Individual Retirement Plans

Some may pose the question, "how do I save for retirement if my employer does not offer a 401K plan?" Or you may be thinking, "how do I build my financial portfolio if I am self-employed?" These are legitimate concerns, and the good news is that there are several options.

If your employer doesn't offer a 401K, your options include individual retirement accounts (i.e., IRA's) and brokerage accounts. Individual Retirement Accounts are investment accounts that are set up at a financial institution and allow an individual to save money for retirement with tax-free growth or on a tax-deferred basis.

The most common individual retirement accounts are Traditional and Roth. Traditional IRA's allow you to make tax deductible contributions. This means you can deduct these contributions from your taxes in the year you contributed, which reduces your taxable income. The contributions are typically invested in mutual funds, stocks, or bonds which grow tax-deferred until the funds are withdrawn. Upon distribution, you will pay ordinary taxes based on your personal tax bracket per IRS guidelines.

With a Roth IRA, the contributions are made with after-tax money and the contributions are never tax deductible. Please note, the taxation of Roth IRA distributions depends on whether the distribution is qualified or non-qualified. When an IRA holder takes a qualified distribution from a Roth account, the distribution is tax and penalty free. For the distribution to be considered "qualified", both the following must be true:

The distribution must satisfy a five-year waiting period (beginning the 1st day of the year which the Roth IRA holder funded the Roth IRA via a conversion or contribution)

-AND-

- The account holder must be of age 59 ½, or
- Have a disability, or
- Be a first-time home buyer, or
- Distribution must be a result of death

Example: Dana started contributing to her Roth IRA in 2017. On February 12, 2022, Dana attained age 59 ½. In December 2022, Dana decided to take a distribution from her Roth IRA. The distribution meets the 5-year waiting period and meets one of the qualifying factors, so the distribution will be tax and penalty free.

Brokerage Accounts

A brokerage account is a taxable investment account that is managed by an investment firm versus a traditional bank. Brokerage accounts allow you to purchase a variety of investment options (i.e., stocks, bonds, mutual funds) to prepare for retirement or simply a rainy-day fund. Although they have limited tax benefits, they offer fewer restrictions and more flexibility than other retirement vehicles like IRA's. With a brokerage account, you can withdraw money at any time with no tax or penalty.

Tax-free Retirement

Tax free retirement is a popular coined phrase that refers to the idea of retiring and accessing your money without having to pay taxes.

Index Universal Life Insurance Policy

Although contributions to your Traditional 401K and Traditional IRA are tax-deferred and reduce your taxable income, you must pay taxes when you take a distribution. Financial experts suggest leveraging an Index Universal Life Insurance policy to supplement your financial plan. Index Universal Life Insurance (IUL) is a permanent life insurance policy that provides a death benefit and has a cash value.

The objective of life insurance is designed to pay a death benefit to the assigned beneficiary upon the passing of the insured. However, many do not know that it can also provide living benefits.

Using an IUL as a retirement supplemental tool can provide a safe hedge against inflation. Unlike traditional investments that are directly connected to the stock market and run the risk of a significant loss, IUL's are tied to the performance of an underlying index. If the index performs well, your policy earns a higher interest rate. If the index underperforms, your policy has a guaranteed minimum interest rate, protecting against a loss in the market. IUL's also have flexible premiums that allow you to increase your premiums or lower them in times of hardship. However, by paying the higher premium, you can overfund the cash value account which will provide a higher income stream in later years. Ultimately, IUL's are great supplemental retirement vehicles for those that have maxed out other traditional retirement accounts (i.e., 401K, IRA's) as it provides a tax-free income stream during your living years, and it shields you from potential market loss.

Health Savings Account

Another way to maximize your savings is by contributing to a Health Savings Account, which is considered the most overlooked retirement savings vehicle. A Health Savings Account (HSA) is a type of savings account that lets you set aside money on a pre-tax basis to pay for qualified medical expenses. By using untaxed dollars in an HSA to pay for deductibles, copayments, coinsurance, and other qualifying medical expenses, you may be able to lower your out-of-pocket health care costs.

Typically, contributions to an HSA are made through pre-tax payroll contributions through an employer; however, you can also set-up an HSA through a financial institution. The only difference is that the contributions would be made with after-tax dollars (money you've already paid taxes on), and you would be able to deduct your contributions from your personal taxes when you file.

HSA's are savings vehicles that offer a triple tax advantage:

1. Contributions go into the HSA tax-free. If contributions are made through payroll deductions, they are also not subject to Social Security or Medicare taxes.
2. You can invest that money and enjoy tax-free growth potential.
3. Withdrawals for qualified health expenses don't incur taxes.
4. Lastly, funds can be used at age 65 for non-medical related expenses without penalty.

America's For Sale!

Home ownership is the perfect completion of your financial blueprint. Real estate is considered by many to be a sound investment that offers unique wealth building opportunities. That is due to it being an appreciable tangible asset; meaning it increases in value over time. Unlike cars, clothes, and other frivolous items that are sure to depreciate over time, real estate almost always appreciates. Homeownership can expand options for the future, whether you plan to sell and make a profit, leverage the equity in your home to pay for other major expenses, or rent the property and create a consistent stream of income.

I became a homeowner at 26 years old, with only $1,250 in my bank account. Until then, I was living at home with my parents. One morning, I was at the car dealership getting my vehicle serviced, and I just so happened to meet a real estate agent. He said, "I see you have a luxury car, but do you have a house to go along with it?" At that moment, I could not help but think my priorities were wrong. As the conversation progressed, we exchanged information. Little did I know this was the start of a fruitful relationship. I was later introduced to his team who were instrumental in my home buying process. Through grant opportunities, I was able to purchase my first home within 3 months. Working with an experienced, credible, mortgage banker is key to determining your buying power, and they can educate you about different lending programs!

Once you have secured funding for your property, a licensed real estate agent can aid you with finding a home that suits your needs.

Please note, it is important to view comparisons of properties in the area to ensure you are not overpaying for your property. Also, reviewing a prospectus of your neighborhood can also provide useful intel regarding the future development of the community. This will support you in making a sound purchase that will benefit you in the short and long term.

For those who are thinking "I can't afford to buy a home", or "home ownership is not for me", my response is, "if you're paying rent, you can afford a home." Indeed, it may not be your dream home, but it is a start to achieve your financial goals. Always remember, if you are renting, you are paying someone else's mortgage without the tax advantages. The tax benefits associated with home ownership far outweigh those of renting. Homeowners can generally deduct home mortgage interest, property taxes, and certain types of home improvement to name a few. These tax deductions help decrease your taxable income, keeping more of your money in your pocket!

As a reminder, the more money you make, the more "Uncle Sam" takes! So, as you're growing in your career and increasing your earnings, you want to find ways to decrease your taxable income by paying yourself first. My tax advisor would jokingly say, "Mia, you have to decide if you want bricks or babies". I said, "I'll go with the bricks for now as this will allow me to take advantage of tax deductions, build my financial portfolio, and create stability which will benefit my future and family legacy!

Be Strategic!

Overall, building your financial roadmap and planning for retirement requires careful planning, dedication, and discipline. This includes an improved mindset, finding a trustworthy financial adviser, and building a team of experts. I challenge you to pay yourself first and invest in your legacy!

If you would like to learn more financial tips, check out my podcast by visiting https://wrna.us The podcast series will provide raw, uncut dialogue regarding the state of "black".

Disclosures:
Information in this publication does not involve the rendering of personalized investment, insurance, tax nor legal advice but is limited to the dissemination of general educational information on financial instruments, products or services. None of the content should be viewed as an offer to buy or sell, or as a solicitation of an offer to buy or sell any of the securities discussed. A licensed, qualified, investment, insurance, tax or legal professional advisor should always be consulted before implementing any of the options presented.

Chapter Twenty:

"Rising From the Ashes: A Tale of Resilience and Redemption"

TROY HOLT, CFEI®, RFC®
Certified Financial Educator

Troy Holt has over 20 years of experience as a sales and account executive. He is a Certified Financial Educator & Registered Financial Consultant Life, Health & Annuity, licensed in 20 states. He is a Maxwell Leadership Independent Coach, Speaker, and Trainer and co-author of an Amazon Bestselling book, as well as host of the Troy Talks podcast. He is CEO (Chief Encouragement Officer) of Troy Holt Consulting LLC, a growing financial consulting company. He focuses on empowering and educating individuals & small business owners on wealth accumulation, preservation, and debt elimination. He is on a mission to eliminate financial illiteracy, particularly in the African American community, with a focus on black women. He is a 33-year member of the same church, serving in ministry for 30 years and as a Licensed Elder with the Pentecostal Assemblies of the World for 26 years as well as Assistant Pastor, Assistant Treasurer, & Assistant Adult Sunday School Teacher. He is originally from Nashville, currently living in Pensacola, FL with wife of 31 years, one adult son, and three grandchildren.

The echoes of my past reverberate in my heart, a timeless reminder of the hardships I've traversed and the resilience I've forged. From the poor housing projects of Nashville, Tennessee, to the uncharted waters of financial instability, my journey affirms the human spirit's indomitable resolve. The trials I have faced and the tribulations I have have shaped the contours of my life, transforming me into the man I am today.

This narrative of scarcity etched itself in my heart, triggering a fire in my belly to forge a different path for myself and those I would eventually be responsible for. My resolve crystallized when I tied the knot and stepped into the whirlwind of married life. A few years in, my life was blind-sided by the maelstrom of financial woes that shook my world. A decision to pivot careers and a 50% pay cut kicked off a landslide.

Passionate and eager, I stepped into the financial services sector. The promised glimmer of a six-figure income within a year blinded me, and I lost sight of the delicate balance between income and expenditure. My lifestyle remained the same, my spending habits untouched, but my income was halved. It was a precarious situation that snowballed, dragging my wife and I into a financial abyss.

Looking back, every adversity was a stepping stone to our growth. We braved the storm of foreclosure on our first house, our dream home snatched away because the payments became too heavy. We lost our brand new car, repossessed due to a neglected car note. Other debts piled up, culminating in the daunting step of filing for Chapter 7 bankruptcy. My wife's wages were garnished for credit card debt, old back taxes resurfaced, and we were even slapped with a monetary judgment.

Each blow was a new lesson, each setback a nudge toward change. In the aftermath of my financial downfall, I stood strong, a phoenix rising from the ashes of its own destruction. I held steadfastly to my faith and determination, navigating through the maelstrom of despair to rebuild my life. As I clawed my way back from the precipice of financial ruin, I discovered a new sense of purpose. My experiences had granted me a unique insight into the struggles of financial hardship—an understanding that could be harnessed to help others in similar predicaments.

My journey of redemption began not only in my personal life, but also in my professional

realm. As a financial advisor, my approach to my clients' needs took on a new perspective—one colored by my own experiences. I listened to their stories with empathy, understanding their fears and hopes, and offered advice that was tailored to their unique situations. I was no longer a mere advisor—I had become a beacon of hope, a guide in their financial journey.

This transformation did not go unnoticed. As I shared my own story, my client base began to expand. People were drawn to the blend of expertise and understanding I brought to the table, and soon, referrals started pouring in. My seminars and workshops began to attract larger audiences, their hearts resonating with the message of resilience and redemption I imparted. The personal and professional growth I experienced affirmed the power of perseverance and faith.

And yet, in the midst of my success, I remained grounded. I remembered the lessons of my past, the sting of hunger and the darkness of despair. I continued to save diligently, ever mindful of the fragility of financial stability. I reinvested in my business, constantly striving to better serve my clients and their evolving needs. Now, as I reflect upon the path I have walked, I am humbled. From the impoverished streets of Nashville to the thriving heart of my financial advisory firm, I have journeyed through life's highest peaks and lowest valleys. I am a testament to the power of resilience, the strength of faith, and the transformative power of adversity.

To those who find themselves engulfed in the shadow of financial hardships, I extend my hand. I implore you to hold fast to your dreams, to seek guidance, and to embrace the lessons life imparts. Your journey may be fraught with challenges, but remember—you are not defined by your past mistakes or your current circumstances.

The road to financial stability is a long and winding one, but with perseverance and faith,

you will reach your destination. Stay true to your aspirations. Remain disciplined in your financial decisions. Hold on to the promise of a brighter future. You have the power to rise from the ashes of your despair, to seize control of your destiny, and transform your life into a masterpiece of resilience and redemption.

Embrace your journey, my friend. Let the echoes of your struggles serve as stepping stones on your path to success. You are stronger than you think, braver than you believe. The potential for growth lies within you waiting to be unleashed. So rise. Grow. Surpass your wildest dreams. You are destined for greatness, and your journey has only just begun.

Years passed since my financial downfall, and I stood resolute on the other side of adversity. Through sheer determination and unwavering faith, I managed to rebuild my life from the ruins of my past mistakes. But it was not just my personal life that underwent a transformation; my professional journey also took an unexpected turn as well.

As I emerged from the depths of despair, I realized that my experiences had armed me with a unique understanding of financial struggles, a wisdom that could be shared with others. I had weathered the storm, learned the hard way, and now it was time to pay it forward.

With a newfound purpose, I embraced my role as a financial advisor with renewed passion and commitment. My empathy for those facing financial challenges became a driving force in my interactions with clients. I listened intently, absorbing their stories and tailored my advice to suit their individual circumstances. No longer was I just a financial advisor dispensing cold, impersonal recommendations. I became a beacon of hope, a source of guidance and encouragement.

The word of mouth spread, and soon, my client base began to grow. They came to me seeking not only financial expertise but also solace, knowing that I had walked a similar path. I shared my story openly, baring my scars to show them that there was light at the end of the tunnel. I became a living testament to the fact that setbacks do not define us; it is how we rise from them that shapes our destiny.

As my reputation as a compassionate and knowledgeable financial advisor grew, so did my business. Clients referred to their friends, family, and colleagues, drawn to the blend of expertise and understanding that I offered. I began conducting financial workshops and seminars, sharing practical strategies for budgeting, investing, and overcoming financial hurdles. The audience resonated with my message, finding hope in the knowledge that they too could turn their lives around.

With each success story, my confidence soared, but I remained grounded, never forgetting the struggles that had forged me. I continued to save diligently, understanding that financial stability is an ongoing journey. I reinvested in my business, expanding my services to meet the evolving needs of my clients. Through education and personalized guidance, I helped individuals and families establish a strong foundation for their financial futures.

Today, as I reflect upon the trials I have faced and the growth I have experienced, I am humbled. My journey has taught me that even in the darkest moments, there is potential for growth and transformation. My hardships have shaped me into a better advisor, one who not only imparts knowledge but also offers compassion and inspiration. To those who find themselves in the midst of their own financial struggles, I urge you to hold on. Seek guidance from those who have traveled a similar path and surround yourself with a support system that believes in your potential. Embrace the lessons that adversity teaches, for they are the building blocks of resilience and wisdom.

Remember, your story is not defined by your past mistakes or your current circumstances. The road to financial stability may be long and arduous, but with perseverance, it can be navigated. Stay true to your aspirations, remain disciplined in your financial decisions, and never lose sight of the promise of a brighter future.

You have the power to overcome, to grow, and to create a life that surpasses even your wildest dreams. Embrace the journey, my friend, and let the echoes of your struggles propel you to heights you never thought possible.

Chapter Twenty-One:

"A Journey in Generational Wealth Building"

PORTIA WOOD, ESQ.

ESTATE PLANNING ATTORNEY AT WOOD LEGAL GROUP, LLP PROBATE, ELDER LAW

With over 10 years of legal experience, I am a Founding Partner at Wood Legal Group, LLP, a family-owned and operated law firm that provides quality estate planning and generational wealth protection resources to our community. As a leader and advocate, I spearhead initiatives that educate and empower historically marginalized communities on how to build and preserve their legacy through estate planning and business development.

I am also a Property Acquisitions Analyst and Legal Consultant at 30th Street LLC, where I use my property law expertise to promote wealth accumulation within underserved communities. I have successfully negotiated and closed multiple deals, resolved complex disputes, and produced comprehensive research reports. Additionally, I am a frequent international conference speaker and media guest, sharing my insights and perspectives on estate planning, business development, and diversity in the legal profession.

Born from the seeds of Enoch George Howard's transformative legacy, I am a living testament to the boundless potential of foresight and meticulous planning. A man once enslaved, Enoch became a beacon of resilience, his actions still nourishing his descendants eight generations later. The enduring power of The Afro American Newspaper, a symbol of collective resistance and vision, resonates still, mirroring Enoch's unwavering commitment to sturdy foundations and prudence.

Embracing Responsibility

As a beneficiary of Enoch George's visionary legacy, I continually reflect on the foundational responsibility it entails. "How am I amplifying and extending this foresighted legacy?" It's a directive compass, shaping the destinies of those who will walk in our shadows.

Foundational Element: Comprehensive Estate Planning

Our transient journey in today's complex financial landscape necessitates a thorough estate plan, marrying our aspirations, values, and loved ones, molding their destinies long after our departure.

Key Takeaway 1: Instigating Property Power of Attorney

Embarking on constructing foundations resilient as Enoch's demands the initiation of a Property Power of Attorney. It's an emblem of control and foresight, protecting our personal and financial realms from court interventions during incapacitating circumstances, allowing us to pre-ordain our protectors in times of vulnerability.

Key Takeaway 2: Establishing Medical Directives

Medical Directives serve as a custodian of our autonomy and decisions, safeguarding our inherent dignity and ensuring our desires are respected and executed, thus keeping unwarranted court decisions at bay. They are not merely legalities; they are declarations of our human essence and the sanctity of our choices.

Key Takeaway 3: Crafting a Strategic Distribution Plan

Articulating a meticulous distribution plan is an extension of our values and affections, assuring our protective embrace encircles our loved ones' futures, ensuring the utmost asset preservation and privacy.

The Symbiosis of Life Insurance and Multigenerational Trust

The strategic integration of life insurance policies for every new family member within a multigenerational trust underlines the perpetual accumulation of wealth. It solidifies the trust as an evergreen sanctuary of wealth, ensuring continual prosperity and financial robustness for forthcoming generations.

Living Enoch's Vision

Enoch George's life is our guiding star, a portrayal of our unlimited capabilities to forge prosperous destinies and resilient legacies. The vibrancy of The Afro American Newspaper, a living legacy, is an echo of this undying potential.

Actuating the Legacy

With such profound inherited knowledge, we hold the compass and the wisdom to meticulously shape our legacies, etching our essence and eternal values through generations.

Concluding Reflections and Call to Action

Our journey is an evolving narrative of inherited sagacity and progressive learning, shaping the lasting imprints we will leave behind. Let's uphold Enoch's timeless wisdom and commit to constructing enduring legacies that reverberate through eternity.

Join us in this transformative sojourn. Start this enriching pilgrimage at blacktrustfundkids.com, a consortium of visionary minds, where mutual growth and collective wisdom paint our tomorrows and forge legacies resilient through time. Let's perpetuate a journey of self-awareness, empowerment, and enduring prosperity, ensuring that our decisions, dignity, and legacies remain unassailable and eternally ours.

Chapter Twenty-Two:
"Creating A Well-Structured Love Letter"

"Acquiring knowledge is pointless if it is not accompanied
by decisive action."

STEPHANIE HOPKINS, BS, ACA, LTA

FLORIDA OSD WOMEN & MINORITY BUSINESS CERTIFIED
YOUR FLORIDA LEGACY BUILDER AND
PROPERTY PROTECTOR

Inheritance of wealth plays a crucial role in providing a strong
economic foundation for future generations. However, the absence
of wills and trust vehicles, can accelerate the loss of Heirs Property,
resulting in a depletion of intergenerational wealth within our
communities, particularly affecting Black, Brown, Indigenous, and
communities of color.

My ultimate objective is to foster an environment where people feel
comfortable openly discussing their wishes. By initiating these
conversations, individuals can begin to assert a plan that grants
them control over their estate and ensures a prosperous future for
their families.

This chapter will highlight the significance of creating a well-structured love letter to empower your legacy. I will discuss how a love letter (this heartfelt missive commonly known as a Will) can streamline the transfer of assets and amplify your voice, to ensure you leave a lasting legacy that reverberates for generations to come.

Craft a blueprint for the gift of your existence to be cherished by generations to come.

My mom was an extraordinary person who radiated sophistication, purposefulness, and a profound respect for God. She was a gifted woman who was comfortable in her own skin, had a fluidless mindset, and was light years ahead of her time in her thoughts and actions. She was a forward-thinker and a highly proactive individual, always anticipating what could happen and devising a strategy to mitigate risks or solve problems. She was fearless and driven to learn and grow, she was never afraid to challenge conventions and encouraged others to do the same. In fact, she had a remarkable talent for identifying people's gifts and talents long before they realized them. She also believed that knowledge was the antidote to fear, and therefore, made a point of discussing real-life issues with her children to keep them informed.

I have a vivid recollection of a particular incident when I was just sixteen years old. My mother had assigned me the task of filing our family's taxes. I protested, saying that I did not understand how to do it. Her response left a lasting impression on me: "The values I am teaching you now will stay with you for life, because I won't always be here to guide you." At the time, I remember giving her a skeptical look and a smirk - after all, I believed that she would always be around. Perhaps it was the immortality arrogance that comes with being young. As I matured, I realized that we arrive in this world with an older version of ourselves, and the cycle of life dictates that our parents won't be by our side forever.

In January of 2008, her words came to fruition when she passed away at the young age of 56. Despite her premature departure, she had already crafted a timeless love letter- a detailed blueprint for her family to cherish for generations to come. By memorializing her wishes on paper, she ensured that her intentions were preserved, leaving no room for misunderstandings or assumptions; shielding us from unnecessary hardships and preserving the unity of her family that should prevail during times of grief.

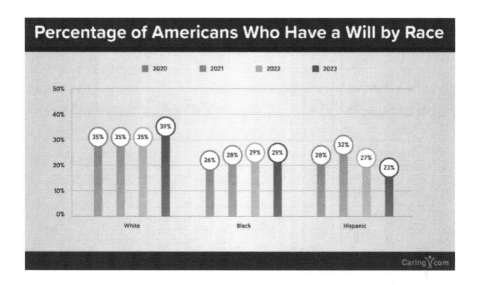

After the celebration of her life had passed, and things returned to business as usual, I slowly began to reflect on the generational wealth that my mother worked tirelessly to pass down to us. I could not help but think about the future of our family home. Growing up with a young mother, I had the opportunity to grow with her and watch her metamorphose into an intellectual powerhouse, displaying her remarkable resilience in the face of life's challenges - including the purchase of our home. She was determined to buy a home to provide a stable environment for her children, ensuring we could continue to thrive in school without the constant disruption and distraction of moving. She also recognized the opportunity in creating generational wealth for her family.

Now that my father was a widower and the sole name on the deed, I found myself wondering what would happen to our family home after he passed away. I did not want my mother's hard work to be in vain nor did I want to have any regrets on not taking action to protect our legacy.

Acquiring knowledge is pointless if it is not accompanied by decisive action.

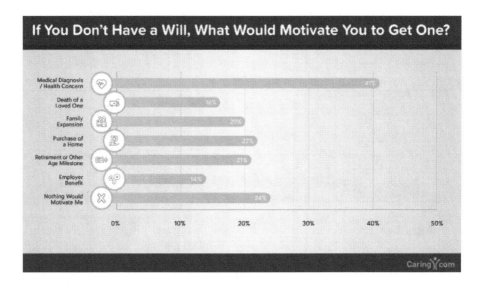

After a few years had passed since my mother's untimely passing, I had completed several educational pursuits, gained mastery over various skill sets, and was making strides in my career, just as she had wanted for me. However, life had other plans. One day, while my family and I were celebrating my niece's birthday, my father had a health scare. He suffered four mini- strokes and was rushed to the hospital; it was a frightening ordeal. I realized then, that I needed to protect the generational wealth that my mother had gifted us. Years later, my father was diagnosed with prostate cancer, but thankfully he survived.

Despite these health scares, it took me six more years to finally put protective measures in place for our family's assets. You may wonder what took so long. The answer is simple: life. Life can be hectic and distracting, with daily obligations and ambitions to chase after. But ultimately, I needed to prioritize protecting our family's legacy and take the time to make it happen.

I utilized a protective measure known as a Ladybird Deed, which is also referred to as an "enhanced life estate deed." This particular type of deed is recognized and approved in only five states, namely Florida, Michigan, Texas, Vermont, and West Virginia. Some states may refer to it as a Transfer on Death Deed or "beneficiary deed".

A Lady Bird deed is an estate planning tool with several benefits. It allows for the transfer of property to a beneficiary upon your death, while providing the following advantages:

1. You can retain the right to live in your home while transferring ownership to someone else.
2. Your home cannot be taken to pay off debts while you and your spouse are alive.
3. Your loved ones can inherit your home without the need for a complicated legal process.
4. You will not have to pay taxes on gifting your home to your loved ones.
5. You can still receive Medicaid benefits while owning a home.
6. Medicaid cannot sell your home after your passing to pay back benefits.

My father was able to use this tool to transfer his property to his beneficiaries without probate, and he still has control and use of the property during his lifetime. Once he passes, the transfer of property to his beneficiaries will be automatic, saving time, energy, and money.

Estate planning may seem expensive to some, but at its core, it is simply the act of making intentional decisions and documenting them on paper about the distribution of your money and property after your passing and who will receive it. Remember, acquiring knowledge is only the first step, taking decisive action is essential for turning your legacy into a reality.

Empower your legacy with a well-structured roadmap that simplifies the transfer of assets and amplifies your voice when you're not here.

Many homebuyers get so caught up in the excitement of buying a new home that very few think about the future of that home, should anything happen to them. Unfortunately, this lack of planning leaves a legacy of financial hardships that many families simply cannot recover from.

Without a Will in place, you have inadvertently granted power to an unforeseen decision-maker: *a Judge.* Your assets will be distributed by the Judge according to the hierarchy of succession laws established by your state. The Judge may decide who will be the personal representative of your estate and even the guardian for your minor children and pets. Leaving the well-being and inheritance of your grieving family to a stranger, may compromise the love they have for you, potentially resulting in resentment.

Financial burdens have been exacerbated by the COVID pandemic and wreaking havoc on the families left behind. The number of untimely deaths, combined with poor planning, has left countless communities and families devastated. Did you know that when your loved one passes away, if the surviving relative(s) reside in the home and their name is not listed on the deed, that they are not considered the legal owner? This situation is commonly referred to as Tangled Title.

This type of title impacts the surviving relative(s) ability to:

1. Qualify for home assistance programs
2. Make payments towards acquired debit
3. Assume mortgage payments to prevent foreclosure
4. Sell the home before it goes to auction

The lack of awareness about this issue is plaguing our communities like a secondary crisis. Education is the cure to preserving intergenerational wealth and allows us to close the growing gap on racial wealth. If you genuinely love your family as you profess, it is essential to extend that love beyond your earthly existence.

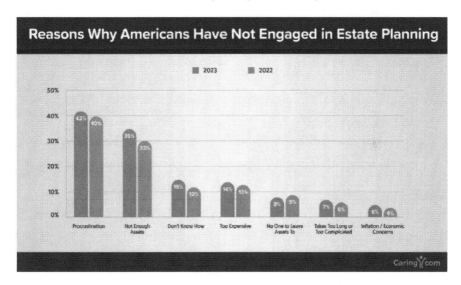

Are you ready to create a simple and cost-effective Will?

Visit stephaniehopkins.wearelegalshield.com, navigate to the Resources section, and gain peace of mind knowing that your wishes will be accurately documented and legally binding. Whether you are from the local area, across the state or even nationwide, we are here to assist you with your property title needs. Visit me at www.stephanie-hopkins.com.

Disclaimers: This information provided in this document is for general informational purposes only and does not constitute legal advice. Business Affiliate: Legal Shield

Chapter Twenty-Three:

"Mastering Wealth Defense: Unlocking the Secrets of Trust Curation and Sovereign Shielding"

DR. TIFFANEY WILLIAMS
Wealth Strategist

Dr. Tiffaney Williams stands as an unstoppable force of nature, renowned for her tireless efforts both locally and internationally. She has garnered widespread acclaim, receiving the esteemed honor of a lifetime achievement award twice, recognized by distinguished leaders including those from the Biden and Obama administrations. Notably, she was recently granted the 44th Presidential Legacy Lifetime Achievement Award during Black History Month, celebrating her exceptional contributions. Her extraordinary accomplishments were further highlighted when she was chosen as one of the recipients of the 40 under 40 Elite USA Global award in New York City. Serving as a member of the Forbes Council for coaches and finance, ForbesBLK council, NSBA trustee, and Council member. Dr. Tiffaney Williams continues to make her mark.

Notably, she earned the title of Global Entrepreneur of the Year, awarded by the International Institute of Influencers in Dubai. Beyond the accolades, her story is one of resilience and determination. Dr. Tiffaney Williams channels her experiences to inspire individuals in correctional and juvenile facilities worldwide, spanning from prisons in Los Angeles to those in South Africa. Her message resonates with hope and empowerment, a testament to her unwavering dedication to creating positive change.

An innovative thought leader, Dr. Tiffaney Williams provides diverse business strategies to emerging leaders and seasoned professionals alike. Her expertise centers on educating individuals about becoming their own financial foundation and mastering the concept of "Owning Nothing and Controlling Everything" through Trust living, sovereignty, and effective business incorporation with expedited business credit options. Her mission is to repair, restore, rebuild, and educate. Her passion permeates every project she embraces.

Trusts are legal arrangements that allow a person or entity, known as the trustee, to hold and manage assets for the benefit of another person or group of people, known as the beneficiaries. There are several types of trusts, each serving different purposes and providing specific protections. Here are explanations for the types mentioned:

1. Irrevocable Trust: Once established, an irrevocable trust generally cannot be modified or revoked without the consent of all beneficiaries. It offers asset protection and can minimize estate taxes.

2. Revocable Trust: A revocable trust, also known as a living trust, can be modified or revoked by the grantor during their lifetime. It helps avoid probate and allows for efficient asset management and distribution.

3. Charitable Trust: This type of trust is set up to benefit a charitable organization or public purpose. It allows individuals to support causes they care about and may offer tax advantages.

4. Beneficiary Trust: A beneficiary trust is created for the benefit of a specific beneficiary or a group of beneficiaries. It allows for the management and distribution of assets according to the grantor's instructions.

5. Business Trust: A business trust is formed to hold and manage assets for business purposes. It can provide asset protection and serve as a vehicle for conducting commercial activities.

6. Privacy Trust: A privacy trust, also known as an asset protection trust, aims to protect assets from creditors or legal claims. It can be used to safeguard wealth and maintain anonymity.

It's important to note that the specific features and protections of each trust may vary depending on the jurisdiction and the terms set forth in the trust agreement. Consulting with a Trust specialist or attorney is recommended for tailored advice based on your specific circumstances.

1.1 Why You Should Have a Privacy Trust?

Privacy trusts offer a powerful shield against unauthorized access, misuse, and exploitation of personal and financial information. By establishing a privacy trust, you can exert control over the use and disclosure of your sensitive data, minimizing the risks associated with identity theft, fraud, and invasion of privacy. Privacy trusts provide a robust framework to ensure that your personal information remains confidential, while empowering you to share information selectively and on your terms.

1.2 The Pros and Cons of Privacy Trusts

As with any legal structure, privacy trusts offer both advantages and considerations to be aware of. On the positive side, privacy trusts provide enhanced privacy protection, allowing individuals to maintain a level of confidentiality and control over their assets and personal affairs. They can serve as effective asset protection tools, shielding wealth from potential creditors, lawsuits, and other external threats. Privacy trusts also facilitate efficient wealth transfer and succession planning, preserving generational wealth for the benefit of your chosen beneficiaries.

However, privacy trusts require careful planning, legal expertise, and ongoing administration. Establishing and maintaining a privacy trust may involve costs, including legal fees, trustee fees, and administrative expenses. Furthermore, privacy trusts may limit some degree of direct control over the assets placed within the trust, as they are managed by appointed trustees. It is crucial to weigh these considerations against the significant benefits provided by privacy trusts.

Secured Party Creditor and Privacy Trusts: Unveiling the Ultimate Asset Protection Strategy

In the realm of asset protection, the concept of "owning nothing and controlling everything" has garnered significant attention. This strategy involves combining the principles of being a secured party creditor with the utilization of living in a privacy trust. In this chapter, we will explore the intricacies of this approach, delving into its potential as the highest level of asset protection. We will examine the benefits, drawbacks, and legal foundations that underpin this strategy. Through detailed information and reputable sources, I will shed light on the concept, allowing readers to make informed decisions.

Understanding the Secured Party Creditor Status

Becoming a secured party creditor involves utilizing the Uniform Commercial Code (UCC) to establish a legal position as a creditor, securing rights and remedies against debtors. By properly filing specific documents, such as UCC-1 financing statements, individuals can assert their rights over collateral and potentially gain advantages in legal proceedings, asset recovery, and debt collection.

The Role of Privacy Trusts

Privacy trusts play a vital role in the "owning nothing and controlling everything" strategy. By transferring assets into a privacy trust, individuals can effectively remove direct ownership, thus separating themselves from personal liability. Privacy trusts add an additional layer of protection by safeguarding assets from potential claims, legal disputes, and public scrutiny.

Benefits of the Strategy

The strategy of being a secured party creditor and utilizing privacy trusts offers several potential benefits. These include:

Asset Protection

Combining the secured party creditor status with privacy trusts provides a robust shield against potential creditors and legal actions. It can help safeguard personal and business assets, reducing vulnerability to lawsuits, judgments, and other financial risks.

Privacy and Confidentiality

Privacy trusts contribute to the strategy by preserving anonymity and confidentiality. By holding assets within a trust structure, individuals can shield ownership details and transactional information from public record, protecting their privacy and minimizing potential targeting by opportunistic parties.

Enhanced Control and Management

This strategy allows individuals to retain control over the assets within the privacy trust while enjoying the benefits of limited liability. They can dictate the terms of the trust, including investment strategies, asset utilization, and distribution protocols, maintaining a level of control over their wealth and financial affairs.

Drawbacks and Considerations

While the "owning nothing and controlling everything" strategy has gained popularity, it is crucial to address potential drawbacks and considerations. These include:

Legitimacy and Compliance

The strategy requires meticulous adherence to legal requirements, including proper documentation and compliance with UCC regulations. Any missteps or incomplete filings can undermine the effectiveness of the secured party creditor status and privacy trust, potentially resulting in legal challenges.

Complexity and Expertise

Implementing this strategy demands a thorough understanding of legal frameworks, asset protection principles, and trust administration. It may necessitate seeking professional guidance from experienced attorneys well-versed in the intricacies of secured party creditor status and privacy trusts.

Risk of Misinterpretation and Fraudulent Schemes

The concept of being a secured party creditor and the use of privacy trusts has occasionally been misinterpreted or misused, leading to fraudulent schemes or individuals falling prey to unscrupulous practices. It is crucial to exercise caution, conduct thorough research, and consult reputable professionals when considering this strategy.

Prominent Examples and Statistics

While specific statistics on the number of government officials or high-profile individuals utilizing the secured party creditor and privacy trust strategy may be challenging to obtain, it is worth noting that the concept has gained attention among certain communities and in alternative media outlets

In the pursuit of comprehensive asset protection and living a sovereign life, trusts emerge as a powerful and versatile solution. Whether through the establishment of a privacy trust or the utilization of the secured party creditor status, trusts provide unparalleled benefits and opportunities for individuals seeking to safeguard their wealth and maintain control over their financial destinies.

By placing assets within a trust structure, individuals can achieve a multi-faceted level of asset protection. Trusts act as impenetrable fortresses, shielding assets from potential threats such as creditors, legal disputes, and financial vulnerabilities. This safeguarding allows for a greater sense of security, peace of mind, and confidence in the face of an uncertain world.

Moreover, trusts grant individuals the ability to maintain a sovereign lifestyle. By leveraging privacy trusts, personal information remains confidential, limiting the risk of identity theft, invasion of privacy, and unwarranted intrusion into personal affairs. Trusts empower individuals to control the disclosure and use of sensitive data, ensuring that they dictate the terms and extent of information shared.

The strategy of becoming a secured party creditor further enhances the protection and control afforded by trusts. By asserting rights and remedies under the Uniform Commercial Code, individuals position themselves as creditors, holding advantages in legal proceedings and asset recovery. This elevated status allows for increased leverage in debt collection and potential recoupment of losses.

While trust-based strategies offer undeniable benefits, it is essential to approach them with careful consideration and expert guidance. Proper implementation, adherence to legal requirements, and ongoing management are crucial to realizing the full potential of trusts for asset protection and sovereign living.

In conclusion, trusts provide the highest level of asset protection and sovereign control. They create an impregnable shield against external threats, allowing individuals to own nothing yet control everything. Through the establishment of trusts, individuals can safeguard their wealth, preserve generational legacies, and navigate the complexities of modern life with confidence and autonomy. As the cornerstone of a well-crafted wealth preservation plan, trusts offer the keys to financial freedom, security, and the preservation of personal and family prosperity. Visit www.whoistiffaneywilliams.com for information.

Disclosures:
Information in this publication does not involve the rendering of personalized investment, insurance, tax nor legal advice but is limited to the dissemination of general educational information on financial instruments, products or services. None of the content should be viewed as an offer to buy or sell, or as a solicitation of an offer to buy or sell any of the securities discussed. A licensed, qualified, investment, insurance, tax or legal professional advisor should always be consulted before implementing any of the options presented.

Chapter Twenty-Four:
"Benefits Aren't Beneficial If They Aren't Understood"

DARYL PERRY II

INSURANCE PROFESSIONAL & HOST OF BUSINESS WITH BENEFITS

Insurance isn't everybody's thing. I help business owners and human resources professionals make sense of it so they can do the actual work they are there to do!

Serving over 248 small and mid sized businesses across the US has taught us how to save companies at least $3,800 per employee in turnover costs.

Working hand in hand with insurance brokers, business owners, and HR professionals helps make this happen.

People make businesses work period. So taking care of your most valuable asset needs to be SEEN and not just a SAYING.

As insurance advisors, our agency provides solutions and strategies for ANY budget because businesses can no longer compete for talent with ONLY a paycheck.

He was shot… wrong place, wrong time just 9 months after I wrote his policy. He was actually my first death claim into my career. This singular day created my tag line of "Have A Plan, Not A Plea." The heinous act was on an episode of "The First 48". I'll never forget his mother, the owner of the daycare he worked at, calling me one afternoon.

"Daryl, I need to file a claim," she said in a different tone than I'm used to. "Sure thing. What's going on?" I said kind of puzzled. "It's for my son. He was murdered this weekend." I paused in silence as I hadn't been accustomed to people telling me that in my past professional life of retail sales.

He was a good kid at just 26 years old and was engaged to be married. He and his fiancé worked at the daycare as a family business. Typically when you think of life insurance sales, most people picture "high pressure". But when this policy was sold, I was talking to his mother and asked a very simple question. "Do you need any life insurance?"

Mind you, this was my first small business account a month or two after I began my career. The owner calmly said "I don't, but my son is engaged to get married so he might need some. I'll get it for him, so his fiancé doesn't have to worry about it." I had no idea how that one question would impact her and the mourning of losing a child forever.

Day after day I talk to employers about employee benefits. Some might ask why, since studies by The Kaiser Family Foundation show that over 93% of firms with 50 or more employees offered health benefits in 2022. Comparatively, companies with 3-49 employees only have health benefits 47% of the time in 2022. When digging further into this data, according to Forbes, about 1 in 4 Americans is covered solely by an employer based life insurance policy.

Luckily the young man and his family were covered. Employers and employees often don't grasp how important employee benefits are to our society and the protection of our finances. When considering the fact that most Americans get insurance through their employer, it should stand to reason that employers should be professionals at understanding this. Big wrong! Overall, 8-18% of Americans understand basic insurance terms. This is not their fault at all as nobody teaches these things in primary school or higher education. As a result, we end up going through life purchasing something usually once a year that affects our entire year and we really don't understand what we bought.

A personal example is my own experience! I grew up a military brat. That meant my insurance was covered by Uncle Sam until I was 21. This made me SUPER ignorant of insurance and how it worked. I remember getting two wisdom teeth removed when I was 21 just to beat the clock and then waiting several years later for the other two, as I didn't want to go through the pain of four at once. No one sat me down to explain the financial ramifications. My own father didn't even know.

Then as I began working in the "real world", benefits were always a chore for the HR person. She would tell me "hey, you need to go to this site or fill out this packet before your deadline passes for benefits." Sometimes I would ask questions and get met with a look of bewilderment and other times they would just say, "look on the site" as that wasn't their job to understand insurance. After all, they didn't have a license or any formal training. So my purchasing process was usually ill informed and a matter of picking "what's the cheapest", so I would be able to get it over with and have some kind of coverage.

This is the experience of most Americans that I've sat down with over the past decade. This is why I believe that benefits aren't beneficial if people don't understand them. To be clear on your understanding of employee benefits, it's not only health insurance. Many people make employee benefits and health insurance synonymous. Far from it! Things like dental insurance, vision insurance, short term disability (*aka paycheck insurance*), critical illness insurance (*think heart attack, cancer, etc and surviving it*), life insurance, telemedicine (video a doctor), Employee Assistance Programs (*EAP*), tuition reimbursement, and more are all examples of employee benefits. Some are obviously more common than others, but employers often don't know their options and most employees don't actually review their benefits guide. Studies have shown that employees take less than 18 minutes choosing their benefits even though it affects a whole year. This pales in comparison to the average 4 hours people spend on choosing a cell phone... Since most employers were employees at some point and probably didn't get anyone to educate them, most of our workforce is the blind leading the blind! HR people are ill-informed, as insurance is not part of HR training.

So what's the solution?

First, understand the importance of employee benefits as an employer. As an employer, it helps to protect your bottom line. The 2nd most expensive part of operating a business is finding good employees and keeping them. The more money you spend on building out people to help build your business, the less profit you'll have. Employers are very in the dark about how much recruiting and turnover is costing them much because that's not a front-line part of running a business. Also, when you don't have tenured employees, you may not have as good of a customer experience. This is due to the "ramp-up" time in education and familiarity with the customer base. Some businesses thrive on familiarity with the customers like daycares, salons, restaurants, and even physical therapy. If a company has a revolving door, customers see that.

Interestingly, there is 1 employer that everyone knows about that touts their employee benefits when they are in the room or not... THE FEDERAL GOVERNMENT!! They do a phenomenal job of seeking out great employee benefits, investing in them, and telling the market what they have when they go to recruit. Although Uncle Sam has an unlimited credit limit when it comes to things serving him, most small businesses don't have that, so they ignore employee benefits. All the while not knowing there are other paths to employee benefits that can literally fit any budget, even down to $0.

Now as an employee, you may want to consider how these programs being provided to you are often greatly discounted to your employer as opposed to you buying it on your own. It is important, however, to read through what is offered. When provided benefits through a job, some human helped the owner select those options. Don't be afraid to ask them for help if you mix up insurance terms like deductible and premium all the time! At least you can make an educated decision on everything offered to you instead of saying no to something you don't understand.

I remember my wife being offered cancer insurance at her job and I had no idea what that was prior to getting my insurance license. Once I understood that it would help us financially in the event of a bad diagnosis, I picked up a plan. Because I knew what it was. You work hard to help your employer, so don't just enroll in the benefits but don't utilize them due to lack of understanding. Not every employer has benefits for their employees so protect your income with these lower cost and typically more robust options.

Over years of countless people contacting me about how their benefits have helped them in a tough time provides me clear evidence of the impact they have. Often I get those messages about the $5 a week policy that the employee forgot and that wasn't health insurance. Employers and employees alike may want to take another look at these "boring" options. They might just be the difference in growing your business or protecting a bank account.

Chapter Twenty-Five:
"Empowering BIPOC Families and Business Owners through Life Insurance"

DR. CONSTANCE CRAIG MASON, MRFC®
Financial Advisor & Consultant

Dr. Constance Craig-Mason, MRFC® is the CEO of Concierge Financial Advisory and the and Investment Advisor Representative at Forthright Capital Partners. As a dedicated Financial Advisor, award-winning Insurance Broker, passionate International Speaker and an x8 Best Selling Author, she teaches her clients to correctly manage their money, so they can live the life they want without worrying about money! She has received numerous awards for community impact in her field including a medallion "In Recognition of Excellence, Service, & Sacrifice" from the Comptroller of Maryland. Dr. Constance has also received an Honorary Doctorate of Philosophy for her eminent contributions to financial literacy, financial advancement and entrepreneurship empowerment. And she was a 2022 honoree of the Association of African American Financial Advisors' 50 Under 50.

Dr. Constance is a member of the FDIC's Money Smart Alliance, National Association of Insurance & Financial Advisors (NAIFA), Financial Planning Association (FPA), International Association of Registered Financial Consultants (IARFC), the Digital Assets Council of Financial Professionals (DACFP) and Strategic Advisor to the Black Women Blockchain Council Board of Directors (BWBC).

Life insurance is a financial tool that provides security and peace of mind to individuals and their families. While it is important for people of all backgrounds, its significance is particularly pronounced for BIPOC (Black, Indigenous, and People of Color) families and business owners. In this chapter, we will delve into the unique challenges faced by BIPOC communities and how life insurance can serve as a vital means of protection and wealth accumulation.

Understanding the BIPOC Financial Landscape

To appreciate the importance of life insurance for BIPOC families and business owners, it is essential to acknowledge the economic disparities and historical injustices that have disproportionately affected these communities. BIPOC individuals often face systemic barriers in accessing education, employment, and housing opportunities, which can lead to lower income levels and reduced opportunities for wealth accumulation.

For generations, my family was no exception to this. In fact, I remember growing up in the inner city of Baltimore, Maryland to a young, single mom. If I can be completely transparent, we lived in unstable home environments, impoverished, witnessing domestic violence and substance abuse. I watched my mom struggle to retain stable work, provide adequate means of the basic necessities and try to improve herself personally and professionally. She was ignorant concerning "how money works." Therefore, the "American Dream" of the nice home with the white picket fence, with the 2-car garage and 2.5 children was certainly out of reach for her and for us. There were no "deep talks" around the dinner table about the benefits of life insurance, or how to save and invest for the future. In her defense, you can't teach what you don't know, right? But it does not have to remain that way. Pursuing financial literacy and applying that knowledge is key to shifting generational hardships.

Moreover, BIPOC communities have historically been denied equal access to financial services, such as loans, insurance, and investment opportunities and have had less access to wealth-building opportunities, such as homeownership and entrepreneurship creating a wealth gap. Discriminatory practices, redlining, and predatory lending have left a lasting impact, making it even more challenging for these communities to build and protect their wealth. This wealth gap often translates into a lack of intergenerational wealth transfer. Given this backdrop, life insurance emerges as a powerful tool to address the unique financial needs and challenges faced by BIPOC families and business owners.

Income Protection

For BIPOC families, income protection is crucial, especially if one person is the primary breadwinner. Life insurance provides a financial safety net for loved ones in the event of the insured's untimely death. The death benefit can replace lost income, cover daily expenses, and ensure that dependents maintain their quality of life. This is particularly important in communities where wage disparities and job instability can be prevalent.

I can remember when my biological father passed away at the young age of 41 years old from complications of a terminal illness, my sister and I were 22 and 20 at the time. Collectively, she and I had 4 young children of our own at that time between the ages of 1-4. Even though our father had not been a part of our everyday upbringing, we still loved him and were devastated when he passed. Unfortunately, he had been injured as a young child causing him to be unable to work and earn a living. He received social security disability benefits along with other low-income state benefits that he qualified for. Needless to say, there was no inheritance in the form of life insurance benefits, social security survivor benefits nor willable assets available for us. We did our best to raise the funds necessary for his final arrangements. It was a harsh truth that we had to accept and take steps to ensure that this was not the reality for our children in the future.

Wealth Accumulation

Building wealth is an essential goal for all families, and life insurance can play a vital role in wealth accumulation for BIPOC communities. Permanent life insurance policies, such as whole life or universal life, not only offer a death benefit but also accumulate cash value over time. This cash value can be accessed during the policyholder's lifetime, providing a source of emergency funds, retirement income, or funding for education or business ventures.

Debt and Legacy Protection

BIPOC families may carry a heavier burden of debt due to disparities in access to affordable education and housing. Life insurance can help ensure that debts, such as mortgages, student loans, or business loans, are paid off in the event of the policyholder's death, preventing the financial strain of these obligations from falling on surviving family members.

Moreover, life insurance can be a tool for legacy protection. It allows BIPOC business owners to pass on their enterprises to the next generation without the risk of losing the business due to estate taxes or lack of liquidity. This promotes generational wealth and economic empowerment within the community. I often speak with my business owner clients about their values, goals, family and finances. Having conversations that allow clients to articulate their intentions for their personal and business assets as it relates to legacy is essential and is a part of estate planning.

Access to Capital and Business Continuity

Many BIPOC entrepreneurs and business owners have worked hard to establish their enterprises. For these individuals, their businesses represent not only a source of income but also a legacy for their families and communities. Life insurance can play a crucial role in safeguarding business ownership and can be instrumental in ensuring the continuity and success of their enterprises. Business owners often use life insurance to fund buy-sell agreements, which dictate what happens to the business in the event of an owner's death. These agreements can prevent disputes, provide a fair valuation of the business, and ensure that the business remains within the community or family.

A key consideration is key person insurance, which can protect a business against the financial consequences of the death of a vital employee or owner. This type of policy ensures that the business can continue to operate smoothly, providing stability to employees and preserving the value of the business for heirs. Additionally, life insurance can serve as collateral for business loans or provide capital for expansion, allowing BIPOC entrepreneurs to grow their businesses and create job opportunities within their communities.

Addressing Health Disparities
Health disparities in BIPOC communities can lead to higher mortality rates from certain diseases. Life insurance underwriting takes into account an individual's health, and BIPOC individuals may face higher premiums due to these disparities. While addressing healthcare inequalities is a broader societal issue, life insurance can provide a layer of financial protection for those who may be at higher risk of health-related issues.

Creating a Culture of Financial Literacy
Promoting financial literacy and education within BIPOC communities is essential for long-term financial success. Life insurance policies can be a tool for teaching financial responsibility and the importance of planning for the future. By understanding how life insurance works, individuals can make informed decisions about their financial well-being and the security of their loved ones.

The Role of Insurance Brokers
Insurance Brokers play a critical role in helping BIPOC individuals and families navigate the complexities of life insurance. Here are some key ways in which they can assist their clients:

Assessing Insurance Needs: They work closely with clients to assess their financial goals, liabilities, and family circumstances to determine the appropriate amount and type of life insurance coverage needed.

Identifying Affordability: They help clients understand the cost of life insurance premiums and ensure that they select policies that fit within their budget while meeting their coverage requirements.

Explaining Policy Options: They educate clients about the different types of life insurance policies, including term and permanent insurance, and help them make informed choices based on their needs.

Shopping for Competitive Rates: They have access to multiple insurance carriers and can help clients compare policies to find the most competitive rates while considering their unique health and financial circumstances.

Addressing Health Challenges: For clients with health conditions, they explore various options, such as guaranteed issue policies, to secure coverage and provide peace of mind.

Long-Term Financial Planning: They integrate life insurance into clients' long-term financial plans, ensuring that it aligns with their broader goals, such as retirement and wealth preservation.

Culturally Sensitive Guidance: Advisors with a deep understanding of BIPOC communities can provide culturally sensitive guidance, addressing potential barriers and ensuring clients feel comfortable throughout the process.

In a world where economic disparities persist, and systemic inequalities continue to affect marginalized communities, life insurance can play a pivotal role in bridging the gap and ensuring a brighter financial future. Life insurance is not just about protecting against the unknown; it's about investing in the potential of future generations and ensuring a legacy of financial strength and stability. The role of an Insurance Broker is indispensable in helping BIPOC individuals navigate the complexities of the insurance industry, address health disparities, and make informed decisions that align with their unique financial goals and circumstances.

BIPOC families and business owners should consider life insurance as a vital part of their financial planning. It offers income protection, wealth accumulation, debt and legacy protection, access to capital, and a means to address health disparities. Additionally, life insurance can serve as a catalyst for financial education and literacy, empowering individuals and communities to take control of their financial destinies.

To ensure that BIPOC communities fully reap the benefits of life insurance, it is essential to address historical injustices, promote financial education, and work towards eliminating systemic barriers to financial success. I encourage you to connect with your licensed Insurance Broker to schedule an Insurance Review today to ensure that you, your loved ones and your business are properly protected from the "what ifs". If you do not have one, send me an email at constance@conciergefg.com and we'll have a confidential, no-cost conversation about protecting what matters to you most! Follow me on all your favorite social media platforms @ccraigmason.

Disclosures:
Information in this publication does not involve the rendering of personalized investment, insurance, tax nor legal advice but is limited to the dissemination of general educational information on financial instruments, products or

services. None of the content should be viewed as an offer to buy or sell, or as a solicitation of an offer to buy or sell any of the securities discussed. A licensed, qualified, investment, insurance, tax or legal professional advisor should always be consulted before implementing any of the options presented.

Love This Book? Drop Us a Rating and/or Review!

Amazon encourages customers to share their opinions to help other potential customers learn more about the product *or book* and decide if it is right for them.

A **RATING** is the *number of stars* the book has. Amazon allows customers to rate from one (1) up to five (5) stars.

One (*not good!*) ↔ Five (*great!*)

A **REVIEW** is *your viewpoint* on the book sharing your thoughts and why a reader should or should not buy the book.

Amazon's algorithm uses the ratings and reviews **to determine the book's relevancy**. *The more ratings and reviews, the more Amazon will suggest it to more people!*

How to Leave A Rating and/or Review?

1. **Log into** your Amazon account.
2. **Go to the book title**, Money TALK$: Uncut Convos with Financial Experts on How to Grow, Leverage and Protect Your Assets. Purchase the Kindle version and read at least 75% of your book before leaving a review.
3. Once you've read the book, now select the **number of stars** you want to rate the book (**Submit**, if not writing a review.)
4. Write your **review*** in the Customer Reviews Section with a minimum of 20 words.
5. **Submit**! Amazon will send you a confirmation email.

* Amazon only allows customers who have spent at least $50 on Amazon in the last 12 months to write a review.

"Subscribe to our Money TALK$ Savings Challenge and Grab Your Paycheck Power BOOSTER Calculator!"

www.moneytalkschallenge.com

Dr. Constance and Anthony Mason

Facebook: https://www.facebook.com/realconnected.co
Instagram: https://www.instagram.com/realconnected.co/
Buy now: https://www.amazon.com/dp/B08XMF4DJ6

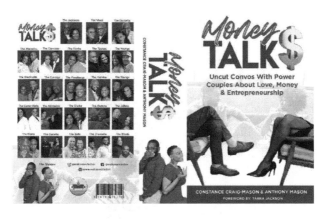

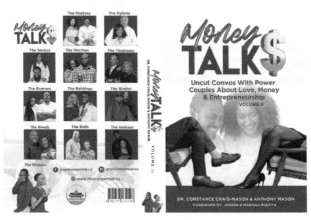

Thirty-five P.O.W.E.R. Couples have come together to share the UNCUT, REAL version of how they have weathered the storms and joys of love, money and entrepreneurship while navigating a global pandemic.

Dennis Kimbro, PhD - Professor & Authority on Leadership & Wealth

Facebook: https://www.facebook.com/dennis.kimbro/
Linkedin: https://www.linkedin.com/in/dennis-kimbro-605a4131/
Buy Now: https://a.co/d/4rmfxVT

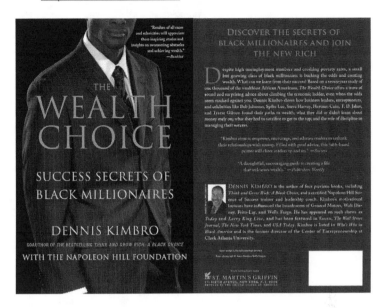

Bestselling personal finance author Dennis Kimbro interviews prominent black millionaires to learn how they got where they are and offers key insights for those struggling to reach the next level.

It's no secret that these hard times have been even harder for the Black community. Dennis Kimbro, observing how the weight of the continuing housing and credit crises disproportionately impacts the African-American community, takes a sharp look at a carefully cultivated group of individuals who've scaled the heights of success and how others can emulate them. Based on a seven year study of 1,000 of the wealthiest African Americans, *The Wealth Choice* offers a trove of sound and surprising advice about climbing the economic ladder, even when the odds seem stacked against you. Readers will learn about how business leaders, entrepreneurs, and celebrities like Bob Johnson, Spike Lee, L. A. Reid, Herman Cain, T. D. Jakes and Tyrese Gibson found their paths to wealth; what they did or didn't learn about money early on; what they had to sacrifice to get to the top; and the role of discipline in managing their success.

William F. Pickard, PhD - Entrepreneur, Philanthropist & Civic Leader

Instagram: https://www.instagram.com/williamfpickardphd
Linkedin: https://www.linkedin.com/in/william-f-pickard-b9a928137/
Buy Now: https://a.co/d/cTLBbbb

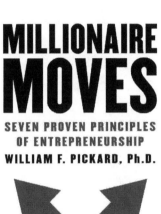

Millionaire Moves: Seven Proven Principles of Entrepreneurship is a down-to-earth, relevant and riveting glimpse into the professional journey of one of the country's most successful black businessmen, William F. Pickard, Ph.D. Dr. Pickard details the highs and lows of his entrepreneurial evolution in an authentic, instructive, and sometimes humorous manner. Young entrepreneurs will be inspired by lessons learned from his bookie uncle, loyal colleagues and determined competitors. They'll also take a little trip through time as he shares the stories of other hard-working men and women who made it – despite the odds. The valuable tips and proven tools provided by Millionaire Moves are essential for anyone striving to achieve the next level of success.

Black Speakers Network - Brian J. Olds, Founder

Facebook: https://www.facebook.com/groups/BlackSpeakersNetwrok
Linkedin: https://www.linkedin.com/company/blackspeakersnetwork
Website: https://blackspeakersnetwork.com

Every day all around the world professionals and entrepreneurs from every industry do something that many people fear more than death. They take one last sip of water, stand up, walk to the front of a room and speak up. Speaking can change your life. Wherever you are on your speaker journey, if speaking has been a life-long calling or a newly kindled interest this book will serve as your road map to the next level. Readers of this book will gain access to the expertise and wisdom of 32 remarkable co-authors who are current and emerging thought leaders, entrepreneurs, and expert speakers dedicated to advancing the mission of Black Speakers Network. In addition, you will find contributions from two titans in the speaking industry, Dr. George C. Fraser and Les Brown, who have both invested their lives in educating, empowering, and uplifting men and women particularly from underserved populations.

Charlotte Howard Collins

Facebook: https://www.facebook.com/coachwithcharlotte
Instagram: https://www.instagram.com/coachwithcharlotte
Website: www.charlottehowardcollins.com

Inquire about this project! Release date: January 2024

Charlotte Howard Collins' memoir is a captivating story of a woman's journey through life that inspires us all to become unstoppable wealthy women. With a wealth of experience ranging from childhood to corporate life, she provides deep reflection and mesmerizing storytelling which openly shares the experiences that have shaped her. Charlotte's story is brimming with honesty, courage, and a raw unfiltered account of her triumphs and struggles. Through her memoir, she empowers and inspires women to take control of their lives, on their terms, pursue their passions, and achieve their goals to redefine what it means to become an unstoppable wealthy woman.

Robert "YB" Youngblood

Linkedin: https://www.linkedin.com/in/YBConnects
Instagram: https://www.instagram.com/ybtheconnector
Buy now: www.CollaborationCreatesCurrency.com

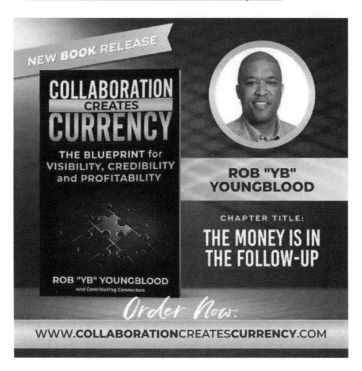

During Rob "YB" Youngblood's pursuit of the #1 Motivational Speaker in the World, Dr Eric Thomas (ET The Hip-Hop Preacher), YB learned a valuable lesson - true success comes through collaboration. Within "Collaboration Creates Currency" YB and his fellow Contributing Connectors share their insight on how collaboration created currency for them, while providing a blueprint that will increase the visibility, credibility and profitability of entrepreneurs, business owners, sales professionals and nonprofit executives. Reading this book will encourage you to think "relationships first, business second and collaboration always".

Lorraine "Coach Elise" Whyte - Leadership Coach

You Tube: https://www.youtube.com/@CoachElise
Facebook:https://www.facebook.com/profile.
php?id=100092867563343&mibextid=9R9pXO
Website: www.iamcoachle.com

Instagram: https://www.instagram.com/mommy_seed/
Blog: https://inthecompanyofmykids.com/
Buy now: https://a.co/d/7AsDxm1

Meet Stevie, an adventurous girl ready for some excitement! Her world turns into a whirlwind of fun when her cousin Jax comes to visit for the family cookout. As they go on an unexpected journey filled with surprises, Stevie learns to embrace her sense of adventure, adjust when things don't go as planned, and cherish the special moments spent with loved ones. Celebrate friendship, family, and the thrill of adventure in The Perfect Cookout.

This book is perfect for kids aged 5-8, and its timeless story will be cherished for generations.

Oliver C. Marcelle - Marriage Strategist & Executive Coach

YouTube: https://youtube.com/denolillc
LinkedIn: https://www.linkedin.com/in/denolillc
Contact: admin@denoli.org
Buy now: https://www.liinks.co/denolillc

In this book, Oliver Marcelle unveils his journey through manhood. Realizing the harmful impact of some 'man laws' on his success, Oliver boldly confronts their constraints, revealing five pivotal lessons that molded his path as a husband, father, and individual. From dispelling masculinity myths to embracing vulnerability and adaptability, he dissects these insights into eight pillars, providing a roadmap for self-discovery. The book isn't a one-size-fits-all manual but a tailored blueprint, empowering men to redefine success in life, career, and relationships. 'Overcoming The Man Laws' is an inspiring guide for those seeking clarity, purpose, and a more meaningful future.

LinkedIn: https://linkedin.com/AndrenaPhillips
Website: KeepMovinWithAndrena.com

Inquire now to become a contributing Author to this project! Release date: December 2023

The Single Mother's Extraordinary Journey "Breaking Barriers, Building Dreams: is a poignant memoir chronicling the remarkable odyssey of a single mother's pursuit of dreams amidst adversity. It invites readers into her world, navigating the intricate dance of single parenthood. Amidst initial shock and societal stereotypes, she emerges as an emblem of resilience and determination. Readers embark on an emotional rollercoaster, sharing her struggles, witnessing her unyielding spirit, and celebrating her personal growth. The narrative weaves the power of love and the impact of unexpected friendships into a transformative tapestry. Ultimately, it's a testament to the indomitable human spirit, reminding us that dreams are achievable, no matter the circumstances.

Lisa Stringer Bailey, MBA, CCRA - Certified Credit Risk Analyst & Financial Professional

Facebook: http://www.facebook.com/lisastringerbailey
YouTube: https://www.youtube.com/channel/UCjERUPn56lOYQR--WqDPZNQ
Pre-order: https://checkout.square.site/merchant/ML62NH07TVNB3/checkout/7MYUQBDA22WSXXJWVL67E466

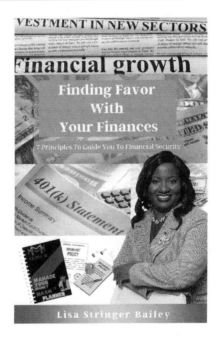

Finding favor with your finances is a guide of 7 principles to financial security. As a financial professional for nearly 30 years, I found myself in a perplexed position. I was over $30K in credit card debt, $40K in student loans, no savings, and the death of not one, not two, but four family members with no life insurance. Talk about a wake-up call!! Jesus and I had a meeting and he gave direction. I want to share my journey so that no one else has to learn how to manage money the hard way.

Kisha Benjamin - Life, Mindset & Empowerment Coach

Facebook: https://www.facebook.com/kisha.benjamin.37
Instagram: https://www.Instagram.com/hittheresetllc
Buy now: www.hittheresetllc.com

Kisha Benjamin invites readers on an extraordinary journey of healing, resilience, and self-discovery in "Surviving Betrayal Trauma." Betrayal can feel like an open infected wound that will never heal, but with time, faith, patience, and the will to reclaim your life, you can survive, thrive, and live your truth! Release the strongholds holding you hostage from the greatness that GOD specifically has for you. You deserve a life of peace, happiness, and freedom, but that will only happen when you DECIDE to HIT THE RESET and TAKE YOUR POWER BACK!

LinkedIn: https://www.linkedin.com/in/drjovanjackson
Facebook: https://www.facebook.com/DrJovanJackson
Inquire to purchase: (800) 747-1839 or
jovan@goodnewsfinancialservices.com

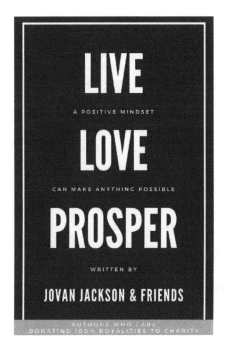

LIVE. LOVE. PROSPER., A shift in mindset can make anything possible", is a collection of inspiring real life stories demonstrating how the authors have dealt with heartbreak, anxiety, pain and struggle in life, and learned to process these emotions to continue their journey towards success. These stories show how resilient the human spirit is, and how simple shifts in the way we think can create massive shifts in how our lives unfold. All proceeds from the sale of the book go towards supporting women's and children's charities in the authors' local communities. We are AUTHORS WHO CARE.

Kimberly Branche - Certified Maxwell Leadership Coach

Awaken Your Inner Warrior is a compilation of "heroic stories" by twelve amazing women that evokes the "warrior mentality" in their daily lives. When life challenges came into their lives, they choose to put on their war clothes and go into battle. Facing their setbacks, loss, disappointments, and turning them into triumphant wins. We know that every day someone is going through a battle we know nothing about. This anthology was created to inspire and empower, but also to help others that are trying to navigate their challenges. Giving them the tools, they need to awaken their inner warrior.

Erica Lane - Chief Profit Coach

Facebook: https://www.facebook.com/globalprofitsos
Intstagram: https://www.instagram.com/globalprofitsos
Contact: cpc@globalprofitsolutions.com

Inquire now to become a contributing Author to this project! Release date: June 2024

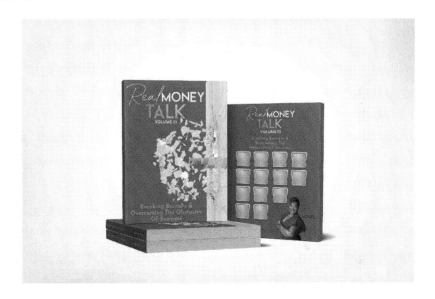

This book will help entrepreneurs shift their money mindset, develop essential profit-making skills, and strengthen their business leadership abilities. The unique feature is the collective wisdom of its co-authors, drawing from a diverse range of experts and seasoned entrepreneurs. Each chapter will not only share inspirational and instructive stories to triumph but will also provide actionable steps to guide the reader. Plus, each chapter will be enhanced with affirmations and quotes to inspire them. The intention is to move entrepreneurs from "stuck" to achieving profitable success. BECOME A CO-AUTHOR and receive training, support, Speak at the summit & more!

Dionne Perry- Board Certified Credit Consultant

Facebook: https://www.facebook.com/profile.
php?id=100064206875721&mibextid=2JQ9oc
Instagram: https://www.Instagram.com/Credit.Lit
Buy now: https://a.co/d/9nVOgnP

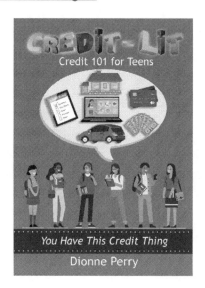

Credit-Lit, an inspiring and informative book, engages teens and encourages them to make GREAT financial decisions. Credit scores impact every financial decision. It's important for teens to understand the positive and negative impacts regarding credit scores and the credit process.

Credit-Lit provides this credit information in an easily digestible, creative format that inspires teens to make solid financial decisions when applying and repaying creditors now and into their adult years and avoid some pitfalls that many adults experience.

Credit-Lit is the recipient of the Mom's Choice GOLD Award - Honoring Excellence in Family-Friendly Media, Products, and Services.

Grace Quarshie - Personal & Business Development Coach {Ghana}

Facebook: https://www.facebook.com/gracebquarshie
Instagram: https://instagram.com/gracequarshiee
Buy now: www.gracequarshie.com

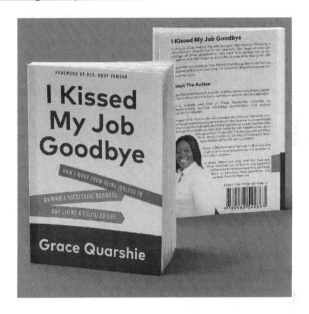

In August 2016, Grace's life was plunged into disarray following a retrenchment program by her employer. She however took advantage of other opportunities and went from joblessness to entrepreneurship and began to enjoy the journey after losing her job. "I Kissed My Job Goodbye: How I Went From Being Jobless to Owning a Successful Business and Living a Fulfilled Life."

Omeakio Tucker - Certified Executive Coach & Consultant

TikTok: https://www.tiktok.com/@elevatewitho
Instagram: https://www.Instagram.com/elevatewitho
Contact: permissiongranted@elevatewitho.com

Your Unstoppable PowHER" is a transformative journey into the depths of inner strength and boundless potential. This empowering book unveils the keys to harnessing your innate powHER, urging you to break free from self-imposed limitations and societal constraints. Through compelling stories, practical exercises, and profound insights, it guides you to discover your authentic self and realize your dreams unapologetically. With each page, you'll unlock the tools to embrace challenges, shatter glass ceilings, and build a life that reflects your true powHER. Get ready to ignite your resilience, determination, and confidence and become the unstoppable force you were born to be.

Otis Togbah Tarwoe- Leadership Development Coach & Business Management Consultant {Rwanda}

LinkedIn: https://www.linkedin.com/in/otis-togbah-tarwoe-634064160
Facebook: https://www.facebook.com/otis.tarwoe.3
Contact: https://about.me/otisttarwoe

Embark on a transformative journey as this book becomes your compass, guiding you toward empowerment, financial freedom, and a life unshackled by the constraints of poverty.

Proudly published by Tebeba International Publishing, based in the USA and Nigeria, this work transcends borders, offering a global roadmap for those daring to dream beyond their circumstances. "Thanks to everyone for their love and support, as this masterpiece will change the lives of many young people across the world. Join me in rewriting the narrative of your life and stepping onto the path of abundance."

Dr. Catherine Jackson - Licensed Clinical Psychologist

TikTok: https://www.Tiktok.com/@DrCatherineJackson
Instagram: https://www.Instagram.com/DrCatherineJackson
Buy now: GuidetoGoodTherapy.com

This guide is what you've wanted to simplify the process of therapy. Packed with information, this book thoroughly explores the process of therapy from beginning to end. All aspects of therapy, including finding a good therapist, what therapy is like, ending therapy, and everything in between are covered in this book. To further make the process less daunting, brain psychologist Dr. Catherine Jackson also includes a wealth of resources, therapy directories, forms, and guides to assist you. Are you ready? Go ahead and give yourself permission to make YOU a priority and get therapy! Your future self will thank you.

Kenyatta Powers-Rucker - Chief Information Officer & Technology Leader

Facebook: https://www.facebook.com/kenyatta8
Instagram: https://www.Instagram.com/DrCatherineJackson
Co-Author Open Call: https://docs.google.com/forms/d/e/1FAIpQLSeGcmpxRgXt_QXgC8hi4XFh8kXbVyuQKArrwpjZU2J8BExWig/viewform

Inquire now to become a contributing Author to this project! Release date: March 2024

"Ladies in Tech: Changing the Face of Technology" is an empowering anthology written by women in various tech positions, each sharing their unique journey and insights. This book serves as a beacon for aspiring female technologists, offering guidance on breaking into the tech industry and advancing their careers. It showcases stories of resilience, innovation, and leadership, demonstrating how women are actively reshaping the tech landscape. By highlighting the accomplishments of these remarkable women, this book aims to inspire a new generation to pursue tech careers and elevate their roles within the field, fostering a more inclusive and diverse future for technology.

Themitha Renee Garner - Playwright & Producer

Facebook: https://www.facebook.com/TReneeGarnerStageplay
Instagram: https://www.Instagram.com/treneegarnerproductions
Buy Now: http://amzn.to/2iVQdvh

In the uplifting self-help masterpiece, *Conquer the Man Monster™ Now, Themitha Renee, affectionately known as T. Renee, invites readers into a world of personal transformation. With remarkable humor and poignant stories of sisterhood, T. Renee navigates the intricate landscape of relationships while unraveling the challenge of self-neglect in the pursuit of pleasing others, including family and romantic partners. T. Renee's narrative is enriched with hilarious tales of sisterhood, drawing readers in with relatable anecdotes that underscore the importance of setting boundaries and recognizing red flags. Through the Man-Monster™ a word coined by T. Renee, she skillfully illuminates the signs often overlooked. This book offers practical self-help tools, nestled within its pages like hidden treasures. These tools empower readers to regain control, establish healthy boundaries, and protect their emotional and physical well-being.

Olymphia O'Neale-White, DSW, LMSW - Licensed Social Work Educator & Consultant

Facebook: https://www.facebook.com/throughmylenseconsulting
Instagram: https://www.Instagram.com/throughmylenseconsulting
Presale beginning January 2024:
Www.Throughmylenseconsultingservices.com

"Survival Guide for Successful Social Workers" was written as a roadmap to help postgraduate social workers sustain their well-being and excel in a demanding profession. This guide will not only help social workers conquer challenges they may face in the field, but also show them how to seize and create opportunities to expand themselves and their brand. Drawing from expert experiences, this guide will share vital tactics and tools on how to maximize your impact, pursue financial satisfaction and solidify your expertise as a professional social worker. *"A Survival Guide for a Social Worker's Success: Student Edition"* was written for social work students to use as a guide as they pursue and navigate their graduate level education. This book offers expert advice from an experienced social worker and provides tips and strategies students can use, not only once they enter their career but right now as a student studying the field of social work.

Dr. Adwoa Akhu - Licensed Clinical Psychologist & Inner Peace Advocate

LinkedIn: https://www.linkedin.com/in/drakhu
Instagram: https://www.Instagram.com/sista.peace
Buy Now: https://a.co/d/4bQV5eu

A simple-to-follow, powerful system that makes it easy to keep stress in check! Women balance so many demands that we often feel overwhelmed and disconnected; Dr. Akhu's time-tested program makes it easy to draw in the positive, clear out the negative, and use even small windows of time to foster mindfulness, clarity, and pleasure in our daily lives, building better relationships with ourselves and others. Countless busy professionals, mothers, and caregivers have learned to decrease stress and increase joy using Dr. Akhu's Inner Peace System. If you are ready to cultivate and sustain inner peace, this book is for you.

Talib Jasir - Dual Certified Life Coach, Podcast Producer

LinkedIn: https://www.linkedin.com/in/talib-jasir
Instagram: https://www.instagram.com/talibjasir
Buy Now: https://www.fwdmovement.org/product-page/say-less-experience

Say Less: Call it Justice invites you to explore the depths of your consciousness and wrestle with ideas of personal freedom. Brought to life through masterful wordplay and lyrical visual design, Talib Jasir takes readers on an introspective journey that bridges critical thought and emotional intelligence.

"Say Less" is an opportunity to reexamine your inner thoughts within over 90 pages of haiku-adjacent poetry, crafted to spark curiosity and awaken the rebel mind. This book is an aesthetically fresh approach to reflecting on society's constructs, challenging your own beliefs, and unlocking your creative mind on the journey towards self-discovery.
Say Less is a three-part experience:

Digital Version (7:54): Consisting of static and dynamic content (Instant Access)

- Mix (55:33): Musical interpretation by Lovers of Now (Instant Access)
- Physical Version (ships in 5-7 business days of purchase)